WHERE DID
MY MONEY GO?

*An Honest Look at Perpetual Debt and the
Fiscal Slavery of the American Family from a
Christian Perspective*

Bob Hopkins, RG (Regular Guy)

WESTBOW
PRESS
A DIVISION OF THOMAS NELSON

WestBow Press books may be ordered through booksellers or by contacting:

WestBow Press
A Division of Thomas Nelson
1663 Liberty Drive
Bloomington, IN 47403
www.westbowpress.com
1-(866) 928-1240

Because of the dynamic nature of the Internet, any web addresses or links contained in this book may have changed since publication and may no longer be valid. The views expressed in this work are solely those of the author and do not necessarily reflect the views of the publisher, and the publisher hereby disclaims any responsibility for them.

Any people depicted in stock imagery provided by Thinkstock are models, and such images are being used for illustrative purposes only.

Certain stock imagery © Thinkstock.

ISBN: 978-1-4497-4031-3 (sc)
ISBN: 978-1-4497-4032-0 (e)

Library of Congress Control Number: 2012902640

Printed in the United States of America

WestBow Press rev. date: 04/10/2012

CONTENTS

Acknowledgements ix

Introduction xi

Chapter 1. Our Real State of the Union 1

Chapter 2. Marketing and Advertising 17

Chapter 3. The Making of a Beast Master 26

Chapter 4. The Beast 42

Chapter 5. My Money Has Wings 63

Chapter 6. The Oppressors 72

Chapter 7. The Ole' College Scam 78

Chapter 8. The Car Payment 92

Chapter 9. The Unholy House Payment 102

Chapter 10. The Credit Card 110

Chapter 11. Taxes 121

Chapter 12. The Lottery 132

Chapter 13. Advanced Cash and Predatory Lenders 137

Chapter 14. Health Care 142

Chapter 15. The Working Mother 154

Chapter 16. What Now? 160

Chapter 17. Giving 179

Chapter 18. Provisions 189

Chapter 19. Truth in a Crazy World 202

Conclusion 216

Resources 223

To Alex,
May you rest in the loving arms of
God's Grace until
we meet again, and what a glorious
day it will be.

To Debbie,
The love of my life, thank you for always
believing in me.

ACKNOWLEDGEMENTS

I would like to take this moment to thank so many who influenced the words herein and those who believed, without a doubt that I would amount to nil in this life and they would have been exactly right had it not been for the grace of God.

For my brothers and sisters in the fire service who give selflessly of themselves placing their lives at risk that others will be assured lifesaving help if ever the need arises.

I would like to thank the multiple writers, researchers, authors and opinions that have given resources in which this book would have not been possible.

And for Caron Miller whose love and discipline set me on the right path one afternoon many years ago. And to all those who have been there throughout a difficult childhood to guide me in the direction in which God's work will be done.

To my loving family who take this journey of life with me. That is, my loving brothers and sisters, father, mother, grandparents, aunts, uncles, and countless friends whose behavior, both positive and negative helped shape my understanding of a Christian world view and rise above the obstacles of life.

And to Alex, my son who taught me what God's love for us is all about, from you I have learned the most. And most of all to my loving wife Debbie who's deep love and commitment to me astounds me each and every day. Thank you for being a witness to my life. You are a virtuous woman.

To God in heaven above for it is he that gives me nourishment, significance and hope that this troubled world is not the end all of things. Thank you Father, for hope through your Son, Christ Jesus.

Introduction

"There is no finer way to destroy a bourgeois society than to debauch the currency" . . . Vladimir Lenin

Most people I know ponder a serious question at the end of each month . . . Where did my money go? It would seem, as Dave Ramsey, author of numerous financial help books says, *"There seems to be too much month at the end of my money."* This problem has become the norm for an overwhelming majority of Americans today and quite problematic. Why? The answers are actually numerous however, there are some basic principles in place in our economic system that are so easy to explain yet mysteriously removed from the average way of thinking. The result . . . a nation chained to debt and financial ignorance.

I was cursed with serious debt for the first 20 years of my working life and clueless as to why. I continued to find myself living paycheck-to-paycheck, making minimum monthly payments, and constantly broke. I just couldn't get a handle on my earnings. I worked hard, obeyed all the rules and considered myself a working-class American that just couldn't get ahead. I soon began to realize I could barely keep my head above water. I would look around and observe people with nice homes, new cars and toys and simply figured everyone else had a better paying job or was just born luckier than I was. That was until I began to understand my lack of knowledge about personal finances and modern systems of money management and realized the pernicious lies that the financial institutions had taught me.

Like most Americans, I believed if I worked hard and paid the bills I would eventually get ahead in life. This may have been true for former generations of Americans, but it wasn't working for my generation and certainly not for me. So, several years ago I set out to discover what was wrong with my generational way of thinking, and through prayer and ample study, I not only discovered answers that changed my family tree but found great insight into a matrix of modern financial misconceptions and misguided ideas designed to enslave us all to a world corporate banking system. I found that I had been taught very irresponsible principles created to keep you and me in perpetual debt which results in huge profits for the banking industry.

What you will obtain in this work is knowledge. Knowledge is power, and that is what I hope you gain more than anything in order for you to reach God's will for your life. Hopefully, what you read in this work will astound you, open your eyes and even make you angry, which may motivate you to take your life back. You probably won't like everything you discover here. You may even feel offended and disagree with some or all of it and simply refuse to accept it and that's ok too. You live in a country where you can do that, at least for the time being. At that I would encourage you to simply close the book and walk away. But some will accept this information and it will radically change their lives forever. Valuable insight awaits those who wish to shake the chains of debt. As Jesus said, *"Let those who have ears, hear."* In other words, a few will get it and most will not, but for the few who listen and begin to apply God's principles to their finances, life will never be the same.

This is not a book about getting rich. It is about finding out why you are in debt, how you got there, and how to get out. It is about simple Christian principles and how they will wake you up to the truth. First, by helping you re-define wealth in your head. Secondly, by assisting you in accepting this key fact: life is hard! Then, it is about explaining the financial powers that use us as pawns in their mega-billions game of chess and how they do it. Next, it is a book of knowledge for the average American family that is drowning in leverage and lastly, it is about identifying the evil knocking at your door in a culture dripping with materialism.

It is my hope and prayer that the information in the following pages will inspire you to seriously consider changing the way you look at money and get on board with forcing our politicians to make the necessary changes we need as a nation to return to the roots of our constitutional monetary system before we slowly lose our right to speak on behalf of ourselves. These times are challenging folks and I fear they aren't going to get any better for most of us.

I am a simple man. I do not desire riches and power. I do not advocate a political party one way or the other and I do not hold a slew of letters behind my name to entice you to believe that I am any kind of expert in anything. With that said, know that I am not a financial advisor, attorney, political or social scientist and certainly not a writer, nor do I hold an esteemed degree from any widely respected university. I am just a "regular guy" (RG) who got fed up with the system of dept and accepted simple fiscal truths that have set me free from the debtors. I have learned deceitful methods of the financial systems and clearly understand the severe damage they are inflicting on people like you and me. I will attempt to expose those lies and share the simple truth with anyone interested in hope that they too will become some of the few who are not indebted to the banking beast.

Now, I challenge you to read on. This work is not about pushing any specific agenda other than freedom through the Christian faith and will hopefully challenge the reader to consider more peaceful and prosperous ways to look at personal finances. We live in a land of vast deception and misguided principles that work to ensnare us into a daily routine where nothing is as it seems. All the while systems and mechanisms of untold power far beyond our understanding work to enslave us. I wish to free as many from that beastly system as possible.

This information is not for the masses. It is specifically for you. If you choose, it will be the beginning of a radical but glorious journey. If you love your family and freedom and believe in a power in the universe more powerful and more important than yourself, then keep reading. If not, just keep doing as you are doing and you'll keep getting what you are getting . . . more debt. Without divine knowledge, you will not be able to avoid it in our current culture. You will be amazed as this will be your first step toward freedom the way God intended it to be. Give it a chance, open your eyes and your heart and learn. Take a step away from the world and the culture of the consumer.

> *"See to it that no one takes you captive by hollow and deceptive philosophy, which depends on human tradition and basic principles of this world rather than on Christ."*
> *Col 2:8*

One third of the Gospel of Christ dealt with evil. Christ introduced the ultimate evil to the world and called him many names but was specific when he exposed him as the Devil. He is a liar and a thief and has been since the beginning of our time. He and his legions come only to kill, steal, and destroy. Jesus challenged us to know the enemy less we fall for his snares and that is exactly what the world does to us financially. This enemy works on every front of mankind and if you do not find yourself wise to his ways, your own nature will lead you directly into his pitfalls. When US Army General George Patton was asked how he was able to outfox the greatest German General of WWII in the North African campaign he replied, "I read his book." General Rommel had written several books on military tactics which General Patton versed himself in. The result was victory over his enemy.

We must study and know our enemy's tactics if we are going to defeat him. It will be extremely beneficial for you to do the same where your finances are concerned. Evil thrives in darkness. Ignorance is born in darkness and lurks there. Yet the truth shines a light upon evil and exposes it and evil cannot survive in the light. Truth is the light of divine knowledge and will prepare you for the battle. But knowledge will not occur through osmosis. You must obtain knowledge through study and experience. Knowledge will be your sword. Prayer will be your strength. Hopefully, this work will assist you in that endeavor. May God deeply bless you with insight to obtain real freedom on this earth.

Jesus tells us, "If you are to live, you must die." This applies to our finances as well. If we are going to succeed in understanding this current financial culture we must be prepared to die to our current way of spending and consuming.

CHAPTER 1

OUR REAL STATE OF THE UNION

"There is one bit of advice given to us by the ancient heathen Greeks, and by the Jews of the Old Testament, and by the great Christian teachers of the Middle Ages, which the modern economic system has completely disobeyed. All these people told us not to lend money at interest; and lending money at interest – what we call investment – is the basis of our whole system" . . . **C.S. Lewis**

WE HAVE A TWOFOLD problem. On one end of the spectrum, we have big banks and the corporations that have grown up around them making record profits via spending by the general population. On the other end, we have a fiscally broke middle-class that cannot curb its insatiable appetite for materialism. Add the two and the result is a bi-polar system with a dissolving middle. This emerging system means perpetual debt for most Americans, placing huge burdens on the working class as well as local, state and federal governments. And in the end, we have a new socialist regime bent on controlling all of it through an evolutionary process to redistribute wealth through a new world order.

The truth is our country is in a mess! Socially and financially and whose fault is it? The answer is much more complex than we

1

may realize but basically, it's everybody's fault. It is the direct result of the self interest of human nature from the executive Wall Street banker right down to YOU! Yes, you and I and our inability to say no to ourselves have brought us to this point. Unfortunately, many ignore all the signs of future hardships and continue to live a life of mass consumption, self-indulgence and materialism.

Most Americans continue to purchase new cars, big screen TV's, new computers, boats, ATV's, electronic gizmos, various other luxury items and vacations in debt up to their eyeballs with maxed-out credit cards in order to have comforts as if nothing has changed. Unfortunately, one day, most Americans are going to wake up to find they are broke and credit cards will no longer bail them out. The party is over and another great depression or something worse could be on our doorstep. If you do not figure this out soon, you will become one of the latest under-class citizens of the new emerging American culture which will reflect only the rich and the poor. The rich, with their understanding of modern fiscal processes will have it all and the poor will be chained to perpetual debt as the practice of usury dominates society.

We have been too ignorant for too long about our own finances and the finances of our nation. As long as we could have our "stuff," it mattered not what the shape of all things were. John Adams wrote, **"All the perplexities, confusion and distress in America arise not from deficits of the constitution or confederation, not from want of honor or virtue, so much as down-right ignorance of coin, credit and circulation."** Once a nation of producers and savers, we have become a nation of consumers and spenders and with easy credit we have spent our lives right into debt hell and, to be more precise, 14.5 trillion dollars worth of debt hell. Perhaps it is time for us to wake up and stop living beyond our means and develop some kind of respect for the workings of our financial situation and understand something about our fiscal problems which affect each of us directly.

Our current situation is at "critical mass," and we have purchased our way into it. But even amid the most turbulent economic conditions, our continued spending has resulted in corporate profits reaching an all time high while the middle class is under siege. So, here's the skinny . . . The middle class is collapsing! That's right! The substructure of the great American culture is eroding at a significant rate. This fact, and I will explain as we go why it is a fact, should shake you to your very core because if you're wondering just what that means, then take a quick glance down south to Mexico, Nicaragua, or any other third world country. That is how we may look in the near future if the average American doesn't stop consuming and start producing again and obtain some sense of responsibility for the mess we're in.

Basically your children will not live the way you do. They will not be able to afford modern housing and nice cars. They will not be able to go to college unless they are willing to sign their lives away to college loan brokers who will keep them in debt for thirty years just to pay back the outrageous cost of a college education. This is how third world countries operate. The rich get richer at the cost of the destitute by keeping them poor, ignorant, and deep in debt resulting in huge corporate banking profits. Because of your debt, you are becoming poor and your children will be poorer.

You may live in a nice brick house and drive a late model car. You may have a garage full of stuff but based on the latest statistics, you don't own most of it. You owe someone so you can have stuff and appear to be affluent. This is a false and bloated system that will sooner or later implode. Because of the money you pay out in interest during your lifetime to have stuff, you live in perpetual debt. This system is making us, in reality . . . poor and that poorness will most likely come to fruition in our children's generation if not sooner.

And what about those corporate profits previously mentioned? They're at an all time high because of middle-class consumption. As a matter-of-fact, the third quarter of 2010 reflected that corporate profits were the highest in US history, according to a New York Times analysis. At the same time, the national unemployment rate reached 9.8 percent while consumer debt has reached nearly 3 trillion dollars and the national poverty rate hit 15.8 percent. As of summer 2011, 40.8 million Americans were on food stamps as the country's credit rating has, for the first time in history, been reduced. Cities, states and the US government are broke and massive budget cuts are going to add to an already problematic unemployment rate. Spending on education, police, fire, national securities, prison systems and hosts of entitlement programs are going to suffer huge cutbacks in the next few years.

Thousands of Americans will protest the cuts as unions and various workers organizations lose bargaining rights, yet none will have many answers to the curtailed spending. Politicians and union leaders will do what they can to save face, but the result will be cuts in spending. Jobs will be on the chopping blocks. But not everyone will be in the debt-filled-poor-house. There is a sector of America who will continue to do quite well.

Those making outrageous profits in today's America are a small select group of CEO's, corporate bankers and financiers, professional athletes and celebrities. This is where your money is going and it is going there because you are putting it there. We want stuff, we want to be entertained, and we want comfort and pleasure and we are obtaining it in mass proportion. We want what we want, when we want it, where we want it, and how we want it. The problem is it all costs money and these people at the top are more than happy to oblige. Our inability to curb our desire for materialism-via-debt is putting us into the poorhouse yet many simply refuse to see that this consumer lifestyle cannot last.

The United States has become part of the global economy. What does that mean to you and me? Well, you can forget a future of unskilled American employees earning $70,000 a year plus benefits working on a GM assembly line, because auto makers can now ship that same assembly line to China and pay their workers $1.78 an hour in a building with no heat to do the same job. What the politicians and the UN didn't tell you is this wonderful world market means lower wages for American employees in order that companies can keep up with worldly corporate demands for cheap labor and huge executive incentives. American owned companies created 1.4 million jobs **in other countries** in 2010. The days of excellent wages plus insurance and other benefits for the average middle-class American worker may be numbered.

Recently I was stopped at a railroad crossing waiting on a train to pass when I suddenly noticed something. No boxcars! I realized that I hadn't seen box cars on trains for some time. Most have been replaced by sea crates, the type placed on ships to China, empty, so they can send them back full of cheap products to be sold in your local Wal-Mart store. As a matter-of-fact, I observed several sea crates with "CHINA" emblazoned on the side of the vessels. In a recent television interview, Donald Trump was commenting that nothing of value is made in America anymore. "It's all made in China," he said. "We are building China up to be the world's most powerful country by our demand for cheap consumer products. Americans no longer make anything yet consume more than anyone else in the world."

For every sea crate that passed by, I envisioned thousands of American jobs disappearing with them. The fact is, and I re-iterate, industry has become global and high paid American jobs for the average Joe are going to be a thing of the past in order that American companies may compete in a world where corporate profits will be the mainstay of all industry. As Corporate CEO's will become more disconnected with the general populace and less accountable as they absorb more and more company profits. The average CEO who grew up in Iowa has no problem living in Hong Kong if that is where the best profits are found.

This fact, along with more government interference, taxation and misguided regulations is sending companies elsewhere in droves and is also killing small business, the backbone of America. Today's corporate climate is all about the bottom line and profits . . . obscene profits, actually, which are gobbled up by a very few at the top of the corporate food chain. In the 1970's, most corporate profits were in the millions of dollars. Today, they are in the billions of dollars for mega-corporations, especially those who bought up their competitors. Many CEO's make unbelievable profits and pay themselves outrageous salaries and bonuses each year, regardless if their companies do well or not. Factually speaking, in today's corporate climate, it is not uncommon for an overpaid executive to run a company into the ground, costing hundreds or thousands of jobs and, yes, get fired for bad management. However, his pink slip will most likely come with a nice "separation package" that will assure him the security of maintaining his lifestyle until he finds employment at the top of another company. All the while, those thousands of Americans who lost their jobs lack a golden parachute and will become statistical numbers on the government funded unemployment line.

More of today's CEO's are simply inhaling millions. The reason for CEO overcompensation is not necessarily greed, but rather a plethora of principles off sprung by our current corporate business culture. The availability of obscene wealth to a few at the top of corporate structures has created a new rationalized justification for this breed of business royalty who no longer consider themselves mortal men, but rather power brokers with oversized egos who no longer believe they have to answer to the same rules as the general population nor suffer the same consequences. When some of the guys at the top are no longer interested in the common good of the public, then public trust dissolves and our confidence in corporate leadership suffers.

In 1970, the average CEO had a 30:1 pay ratio compared to the average line worker. Today, that average is between 300:1 and 500:1. One particular president of a major bank was paid one thousand times the salary of his average bank teller and in a recent interview, had absolutely no problem with the situation and believed every penny his just reward. No middle class structure will ever be able to survive such an arrangement. The rich continue to get richer because of exuberant corporate profits and the poor continue to get poorer because of debt as pay schedules for the average American middle class employee remain flat while being devoured by inflation and taxes. On average, CEO pay scales rose approximately 400 percent between 2003 and 2007.

As a result of this corporate trend, Americans recently witnessed something completely out of line with our constitution. While we were asleep, the US government took over the banking business among others. The event was not only historic, bold and believed necessary by the current administration but was a very, very dangerous venture and a huge threat to what is supposed to be a free market economy. The unscrupulous and sometimes unlawful practices of the US banking system lead to the takeover of the big banks and various financial institutions as a direct result of years of deregulation and trickle-down economics, (which stopped trickling), but a government takeover of any business may be something we all come to regret. It was extremely ironic that the most liberal President in American history who ran on the promise of change gave billions of dollars to the very scoundrels who have historically exploited the poor and working class. And he did it as one of his first acts in office.

As a result of years of deregulation in the banking system coupled with government intervention and social pampering, the financial industry was out of control. The mis-management within their ranks became a huge debt problem for the populace as interest craving investors crowded Wall Street. This national debt frenzy was a free-for-all for the banking institutions as a direct result of their ability to create millions of bad loans for people and companies who couldn't afford them while ignoring the warning signs of impending doom of massive proportions.

Wall Street's years of irresponsibility coupled with unscrupulous greed in the derivatives market (stocks made from nothing to make the rich filthy rich) had caught up to it, and some of the big banks unregulated loaning practices were leaving them unstable as several began to realize they were in trouble. The bow had to break and when it did, a fully Democratic controlled administration saw their chance to socialize the banking industry and forced the Wall Street fat cats to take a bail out (of our tax dollars) of unspeakable sums. Though some of the banks, such as Wells-Fargo, declined the offer, there was ultimately no choice in the matter. 800 billion US tax dollars were transferred into the private banking sector, and Uncle Sam was now in the banking business, or so it appeared. But further investigation into the practice began to reveal an interesting fact. Some of the same people who regulate our governmental financial systems seem to be the same people who work in the Wall Street banking institutions and vice-a-versa. In other words, several key players tend to operate back and forth in both sectors and have for years. Perhaps the fox has been designing the hen house way too long!

One would be inclined to believe that Wall Street would be licking its wounds after the collapse of 08, but the bail out only acted as an enabling tool that simply allowed the banksters to continue their insatiable addiction. Bonuses on Wall Street were up by 17% in 2009 while factories, local businesses, and municipalities were cutting employees and services. On top of that, another 140 billion dollars was funded to the banking system, virtually unnoticed by the general public, as banks were allowed for the first time, to buy up failing businesses. Federal employees also saw pay hikes as growth in their job sector was observed in 2009. In a direct and indirect way, these two power hounds will affect the way we live as Americans. The good times are over and change has definitely taken place, some good but most bad. A fact of history is that every great culture or society has decomposed because of two main factors . . . over taxation and immorality and today's financial system is definitely immoral as

Uncle Sam and his offspring, state governments, continue to tax us to death. Considering all that has taken place over the last 100 years, we have set ourselves up for a major let down.

It is very important that we understand how we got here. It didn't just happen overnight. According to Dr. Elizabeth Warren, former Professor of Bankruptcy Law at Harvard University, in her book, <u>The Two Income Trap</u>, "Salaries for the average American worker have flatlined over the last 30 years while corporate profits have skyrocketed." In 1965, the average family only needed one income. Dad could earn a living, make the house payment, the car payment, feed and clothe the family, along with medical expenses, and take the entire family on a vacation every year and he still had enough left over to save. Then something happened. Prices began to rise due to inflation in the early 1970's when Wall Street speculators created the false impression that the world was running out of certain items such as coffee, tea and sugar. Soon, oil and energy were encapsulated into the big fib, and prices began to rise quickly. They never came down even though average folks figured out there were no shortages on any of those items. Now, with a higher cost of living and a change in our social climate, Mom entered the workplace. One would think that such a move would have doubled a family's annual income, but such wasn't the case.

Today we see the need for both Mom and Dad working to make ends meet, or so it may seem. Why? Dr. Warren found through statistical analysis that huge changes in our cost of living took place over one generation of time. From 1970 till today:

1. House payments are up 76%
2. Health Insurance is up 74%
3. Automobile costs are up 54%
4. Taxes are up 25%
5. Childcare is up 100% (childcare, for the most part, did not exist in 1970)
6. College tuition is up approximately 865%

One thing that Professor Warren points out is the fact that consumer items, based on the rate of inflation have actually gone down because of availability; however, I have discovered that the way we pay for those items is through credit cards or revolving debt, which did not exist in the average American home in 1970. With that said, let it be noted that credit card debt is also considered to be up by 100% as our basic standard of living has quadrupled over the last fifty years.

This is now our reality, and it only gets worse as debt has become king. Your household most likely operates in debt, your city operates in debt, your state operates in debt, and the US government operates in debt. Everyone has more money going out than coming in. This cannot continue as certain laws of physics will bring it all to reality at some point, possibly in a violent way.

Below are the latest statistics concerning our social crisis regardless that the current administration is reporting that our situation is improving. They, just like the former administration, are telling us to get out and spend money to help the economy. The simple truth is, nobody ever spent their way out of debt. Just do the math. We cannot and will not spend our way back to a strong economy. Not ever! The American dream has become our nightmare. Debt has become so ingrained into our culture that "we can't imagine a car without a note, a student without a loan, a house without a mortgage or credit without a card," reports Dave Ramsey, author of the book <u>Financial Peace University</u>. The following statistics reported by government statistical analysis offices and various other financial and social reporting agencies tell a grim story:

- Our country is now over 14 trillion in debt.
- Because of our national debt, our national credit rating has now dropped from AAA to AA+ for the first time in American history.

- The US government is printing money daily, and the interest paid on that money is obscene.
- We have created a system based on debt. If there were no debt, we would starve, and we are dependent on a debt system.
- 83% of US stocks are now owned by the top 1%.
- 66% of income growth from 2001-07 went to the top 1%.
- 36% of Americans now contribute absolutely nothing to retirement or savings.
- 43% of Americans now have less than $10,000 saved for retirement.
- 24% of eligible Americans postponed their retirement in 2009.
- 1.4 million Americans filed for bankruptcy in 2009, up 36% from 2008.
- Only the top 5% of Americans have earned enough to match the rise of housing costs since 1975.
- As of 2007, the bottom 80% of American households held only 7% of the liquid financial assets.
- The bottom 50% of Americans now "collectively" own less than 1% of the nation's wealth.
- The average Wall Street bonus was up 17% in 2009 from 2008.
- The top 1% of Americans now own nearly twice as much of corporate wealth as they did in 1995.
- More than 40% of Americans are now working in low paying service jobs.
- More than 40 million Americans are now on food stamps and according the US Department of Agriculture, that figure could rise as high as 43 million in 2012.
- 21% of American children live below the poverty line.
- The top 10% of Americans earn over 50% of the national income.

- More families filed for bankruptcy in 2010 than did for divorce.
- Approximately 76% of Americans say that debt is severely impacting their lives.
- 61% of Americans live paycheck to paycheck.
- Mortgage debt has more than doubled since 1990.
- Approximately 2.1 million Americans lost their homes to foreclosure in 2011.
- The typical bankruptcy is a middle class, college degreed baby boomer with extensive credit card debt.
- 15.4% of American adults now live below the poverty line.
- 59% of Americans could not cover one month's expenses if they lost their job.
- The typical American family has approximately $38,000 in consumer debt and that does not include the mortgage.
- The credit card industry mails out approximately 4 million credit card applications each year in the United States alone.
- 67% of Americans do not pay off their credit card balance each month.
- 69% of bankruptcy filers claim that credit card debt was the main culprit.
- The average American household owes 187% more than it did in 1990.
- Food prices are on the rise as corn has risen 76% in 2011.
- Sugar has risen 167% and soybean 46%.
- Real median household income has dropped 0.7%
- Food stamp recipients have increased by 35.1% since 2009.
- The number of unemployment recipients has increased 22.2%.
  . . . and the list goes on as the rich get richer!

Professor Warren said, *"Capitalism is the most productive economic system ever created. I am not suggesting that we abandon it, but our society unquestioningly subordinates everything to profit and when it includes our food, our news, our vehicles and our earth, then maybe it's not good to see it through corporate America's eyes."*

The average American is completely out of sorts with money or how to handle it. But the big banks understand it very well. Basically, it works like this: if a person makes an average of $50,000 annually he will make approximately 1.5 million dollars in his lifetime. Let's say, for sake of argument that he lives in a new home that he built for $200,000. In that case, his $200,000 loan is actually a $383,000 loan, after interest for 30 years is added. He will spend almost a third of his life's income paying for that home. Then he will spend another one third of his life's income paying taxes. Lastly, he will actually keep about $500,000 of his 1.5 million earnings over his lifetime. That is what he will live on. That is to pay for medical expenses, send the kids to college, food, clothing, transportation, insurance, etc., for an entire life's wages. Once again, the math doesn't add up, so in this current system where the average person is totally ignorant of how to keep his money, he will never have enough and will have to depend on debt (mainly credit cards, car notes and student loans, etc.) to survive or at least to obtain the goods he has been convinced he needs. Basically, he lives above his means. No matter how broke he is, he will still drive a new car with high monthly payments. The banksters love this fact as it is this perpetual debt system that continues to make them richer and richer. The system was actually designed to work this way and we will see how it all comes together in another chapter.

Unfortunately, in this system we have generational debtors. One's grandparents lived by debt, the children will learn to live by debt, and the system perpetuates itself to create a class of people that can never rise above their current situation. Basically, this is how generational slavery works. A mental ball and chain around the family tree, from one generation to another to the point that a generation is born that not only misunderstands freedom but couldn't function in it anyway and will forever demand available government assistance to survive.

Just like taming an elephant, simply tether a back leg to a stake in the ground when he's a baby so he can't get away. As he grows, he stops trying, as he believes he can't and gives up hope. Even though, once he is full grown and could easily break the rope, he doesn't even try because he has been taught a belief system convincing him that he must stay tied to the stake forever and forever a slave to his own belief. Generational debt works the same way. Mom and Dad live in debt, so the children believe that too is their only way to obtain stuff. And they have learned that obtaining stuff is what life is all about.

My great-grandfather was poor, my grandfather was poor and my father was poor so naturally, I too was en-route to a life of poor. When I was 7 years old, my father disappeared in Viet-Nam further deepening our poorness. Fortunately, we lived in a small town where everyone knew everyone else, and I had several siblings so we were blessed with many friends. Even as a child I became aware of how poor we were every time my mother reminded me. I did not want to be poor and ignorant so I began to observe middle class families, mostly those of my friends. I watched how they operated, the rules in their homes, their values, the way they viewed life, etc. I wanted to be middle class so I began to think and do like the middle class. Once I obtained that lifestyle as an adult I found myself in debt just like the middle class. So I began to wonder how the wealthy think and began to study them and found they have a different opinion of debt than do the middle class. It was time for me to think like the wealthy . . . first by understanding that wealth doesn't mean stuff. *It means freedom from debt.* Wealthy people are not those who surround themselves with materialism. Rather, they are people who understand freedom because they are free from debt. Freedom is their life goal. Debt free resulting from fiscal knowledge and responsibility is the foundation of wealth and a true blessing from God.

But, I then discovered a problem. We have a system in this culture. It is a feudal system of debt, and it absorbs everyone and forces Americans to live by the skin of their financial teeth. Debt is everywhere and almost every family is one paycheck away from bankruptcy. The loss of a job or a major medical diagnosis could bankrupt the average American family in a matter of weeks or months. My new way of thinking had to be radical and totally different than the average American, so I had to live beyond the expectations of average and attempt to live a life that was independent as possible of credit cards, mortgage companies, auto financers, department stores, and any other banking institution out there. I had to figure out a way to live without them or at least make them work for me on my terms, not theirs. I had to get a step ahead of this system and free myself from the predator banks and other financial institutions. If I did not change my way of thinking, I would continue to repeat my actions. As history tells us, those who do not learn from their mistakes are sure to repeat them. And historically, the average person continues to make the same financial mistakes over and over again. I knew I had to think different and learn from history.

By the 4th century, Rome had fallen. It's once great society collapsed basically for many of the same reasons as our own and along with it went the arts, culture, safety and prosperity which catapulted the western world of that day into the abyss of the dark ages. Governments and armies slowly weakened and dissolved no longer existing to protect the people and war and anarchy became rampant. Over time, emerging European kings evolved and created a system in which they contracted or appointed new lords or landowners in order to protect their kingdoms. These lords (mostly relatives or pals of the king) would allow the general populace ownership of small fractions of lands within their kingdoms for the promise of security by knights who were appointed or knighted by the lords or the king to protect the realm. The only problem with this contract is the populace, called serfs or peasants, were required to give up 50 to 80 percent of what they farmed or produced to the lord via taxes or serve as conscripts in his army. This system worked for about a thousand years and through it kingdoms were born and wealth was made for the nobles (the small group on top of the social structure). It wasn't so good for the peasants as they worked and toiled daily, producing but never truly reaping the rewards of their labor as they would always be indebted to the "Lord of the Land," basically living as slaves.

Another drawback for the peasants was they could never rise out of their poor situation nor could their children. If one was born a peasant, it was likely that he would die a peasant. Today, we see a system developing in America quite like the old European feudal system. The only thing that has changed is the names. Instead of King George, we have King Visa and instead of Lord Hamilton, we have Lord MasterCard.

If the current banking system has its way, all those in debt will remain in debt in order that the system can continue, keeping the very wealthy, very wealthy. The problem is, it keeps those in debt in a constant state of debt and with no middle class, there will be no way out of that debt. The debt monster (the beast) will perpetuate the situation and keep the general population in bondage and it makes no difference if you are a doctor or a day laborer, your lifestyle of indoctrinated consumption will keep you loyal to the beast. As we will see in the next chapter, the beast has convinced you that you need him.

. . . "and the borrower will become slave to the lender".

CHAPTER 2

MARKETING AND ADVERTISING

"Go on and buy that luxury automobile and set yourself apart from the rest, after all, you deserve it"

ONE SATURDAY MORNING IN the 10th year of my youth, I was sitting in front of the TV enjoying a bowl of my favorite sugar-coated cereal watching Scooby Doo. Then I saw it in a commercial. The coolest, newest and most sensational toy a boy could ever wish for. "The Speedy Super Track" made of bright orange plastic with the loop-de-loop. I just had to have it or else I would die. Soon, Christmas morning arrived and sure enough . . . I got just what I wanted. The toy I anticipated for so long was now mine except nothing worked for me the way it worked for the kids in the commercial. I found the track impossible to use in the house, and the cars wouldn't stay aligned the way they did on TV, and that cool loop de loop was most disappointing. After a couple of hours I became very bored, frustrated, and disappointed with the whole thing and crammed it all back in the box. In the closet it went, never to be used again. At the time, I figured I must be an idiot because the kids on TV didn't have the problems with the toy as I did. Surely they didn't lie; after all, it was on TV.

Eventually, even as I child I realized I had been hoodwinked by an ideal marketing campaign designed by very smart people who were counting on my ability to influence my parents into spending their hard-earned dollars on a useless toy that a commercial convinced me I just had to have. But don't be fooled into believing that this process only applies to children. It happens to us adults, too; every hour of every day and marketing firms are counting on it.

The truth is, there is little honesty in modern advertising, and everyone in America thinks they are exempt from the influence of it. Think again! There is an old saying that the best trick the devil ever played on the world was convincing it that he doesn't exist. The world is designed to take your money, and it does so every day by advertising through mass media. Most people are completely clueless that they are victimized by this scheming devil on a consistent basis. Modern advertising, with the help of technology is in your face, all day-everyday. Unlike ever before, it is everywhere you look, everywhere you go, and involved in almost everything you do. It is the purpose of this system to sell product and create a cradle-to-grave consumer. The more money advertisers and marketers can squeeze from the basic consumer, the more money they make and they make a lot of money. Advertising has become a major money making business throughout the world. Advertising executives are some of the best paid people on the planet in this 180 billion dollar a year business.

No one is immune to advertising, unless you live in a cave on the river, and even there discarded trash will eventually float past you with a major brand name staring you right in the face. The average American is bombarded with over 3,000 advertised images daily and will spend three years of his life watching commercials on television. Most people watch TV and never realize that one third of a one hour program is taken by paid commercial spots. A one hour show is only a forty minute show, or less. Images come to us from every angle and are designed to permeate every sense of our body through smell, taste, sight, feeling and hearing. What's worse is the fact advertising subversively goes far beyond what we realize.

Advertising sells! And it sells a lot more than simply product. It sells love images, concepts of sexuality, romance, success, beauty, and a concept of "normalcy" to a generation of Americans who lack a moral compass. It is attempting to tell us who we are and who we should be. It tells us how we should look, especially women. Each year thousands of young girls die from eating disorders because they have believed some distorted advertised lie that they are too heavy and the girls in the magazines and on TV are all thin, ridiculously thin, but media tells us that is just how girls should look.

Some advertising and marketing firms hire sociologists, research scientists, behavior therapists, psychologists, psychiatrists, biologists and various other social scientists to gather as much data as possible as to how the human mind works, what it wants, what it craves, and how it can be convinced to purchase products. Marketing companies set out years ago to create "mental associations" to entice people to buy certain products. This concept in advertising began shortly after WWI when advertising specialist understood the importance of an emotional connection where products were concerned. They figured out that they could better sell products to people if there was some kind of psychological connection between the product and the consumer. The mental association still works today, especially with something we already feel good about such as "our children's favorite restaurant" or "some cuddly character" or a host of commercials that target the emotional side of your senses to sell you something. This social conditioning is designed to create an automatic response in a person. These are called behavior modification techniques and are commonplace in the business. They are transferred via radio, television, smart phones and other means of technology.

What about exploiting our children? Our modern environment is created via mass media designed to sell products by creating a world view in which consumerism is the key element. Simply put, consumers are marketed and manipulated into buying products, and families are completely unarmed and unprepared to combat such a huge monster. The industry has created "cradle-to-grave" consumers, and the majority of American parents are completely oblivious to it. The new goal of marketers is to institute their client's name brands into the lives of children to assure life-long consumers during the informative years of their lives. Marketing has become quite aware of the fact that there are 52 million children under the age of 12 in America today, and those kids have spending power. Fifty years ago, the average kid may have had two cents on him if he were lucky, but today children receive money as allowance, for birthday gifts from grandparents, parents and friends and family, but most of all, these kids have influence over the people who do have a lot of purchasing power . . . their parents.

Advertisers know that the real money is in a child's purchasing influence over Mom and Dad and have made it a point to make parents miserable. Why do you think the candy is always at the check-out stand? It has been documented that marketers have even performed studies on which tantrum by children works the best and the best product to trigger that very behavior. At some point, the average parent gives into the child who is constantly under the influence of the "want."

No other generation has been manipulated like our current one. The massive marketing campaigns that take place today happen on a huge scale in order to hook as many consumers as humanly possible. Our kids are being marketed to more than ever. There is some kind of brand name shoved in front of them 24 hours a day. An encircling subversive marketing campaign has been designed to capture every desire they may feel in order to create an army of loyal consumers, and it is working like a well oiled machine. Our kids are buried in a media blitz 24-7 as they are now wired in, literally, via I-phones, computers, Internet, TV, etc., and brand loyalty is the marketing goal, to teach them young that life is all about buying, about getting, about owning, about self, about me and gluttony. You've just got to have stuff, stuff, and more stuff.

"Cradle-to-grave" simply means get them early and often. It starts while they're still in the womb. And crazy as that sounds, one marketing CEO was reported saying that "children in the womb are the future of America and the most important consumer there is." Don't believe me? Just try to find disposable diapers without some kind of cute little, snuggly character affixed on them. Almost every item a baby is wrapped in has some major cartoon character labeled on it, and those little characters mean big bucks for executives. Look at toddlers and see what they wear. Name brand or media characters are all over them.

In 1973, the Senate hearings on advertising to children took place in Washington D.C. Peggy Charman, a leading child advocate of that time, reported that advertising to children was a deceptive practice and should be stopped. Most sociologist and children protection groups agreed. However, in 1980 the Federal Trade Commission Improvement Act outlawed the commission's authority to regulate corporate advertising to children. Since then, marketing to children is up 852 percent with a 35 billion dollar increase in sales. The emotions of children have been turned into profits. Today we see that advertising focused on movies, video games, cartoons, children's programming, etc. Advertising must get to the kid at all costs in order to create a consumer cadet with no moral restrictions or fiscal boundaries as these organizations have become predators for the minds of our young.

Marketing classes in today's universities are part of the beastly system as well. With advanced academic research programs designed to indulge marketing students with new tools like Internet micro-targeting that gathers as much information on consumers, especially children, as possible in order to create a continued marketing program based on the individual consumers wants. Young consumers are being studied under the microscope in order that corporate marketers may reach them in every aspect of life. Fine tuning techniques are now being used to reach every age group to see how certain products can get to them. Social scientists and biologists are being integrated into the marketing research labs in order to probe the minds of people, known as "neuro-marketing". It is used to probe neurons in the brain to test the reactions of consumers with certain behavior patterns based on desire and need. By using neuro-marketing" advertisers can discover what subconsciously appeals to the consumer, especially children, by studying eye movement, body temperature, muscle reaction and the like in relation to certain products in order that the corporations may better move those products.

And now, there is a new kid on the block, a new idealism in marketing. An undercurrent of today's mental regime has a new tool at hand that is more subversive and dangerous than any other. It is "value marketing"- placing value on an individual based on the products that they purchase. What you purchase now has social meaning alone. What you buy is who you are. In other words, it defines who you are as an individual and how others will accept or reject you. You are what you buy and if you don't have it, you are less than nobody . . . you are not cool. This is especially effective with younger generations primarily in elementary and middle school grade students. It is not product that is being marketed but value. It is stuff! Self indulgence, instant gratification and materialism. It's all about me. I must have it if I am ever going to count. Advertising has moved into one of man's most vulnerable places: the search for significance.

This form of advertising does not only affect the young. Look around! What kind of vehicle do you drive? Why do you drive it? Where do you live and why do you live there? Where do you go on vacation? What kind of clothes do you wear? What kind of make-up do you buy? What college or professional sports teams do you like and why? Who do you choose as friends and associates? It can even determine where you go to church and why you go there. And you just thought you had freedom of choice. The truth is, for many, corporate America has been telling you who you are and how to spend your money since you were a child.

Mike Catherall of the American Chronicle said it best in his ethics piece on certain companies advertising unethical elements; however, I believe his article can easily be said of all modern advertising concepts everywhere.

He said, "There are plenty of things out there to buy and for everything that is sold there is a sign somewhere advertising that product and words of mouth spreading the news of that product to someone else. Whenever there is something to be traded there is talk and wherever there is talk there is advertising.

For every human desire there is an answer. Often this manifests itself in vice, sin or what-have-you. The presence of most of these objects in the world is not evil in their own right. There are dangerous things out there, but their availability is not the issue at least in this context. It is the manner in which dangerous things are encouraged that needs to be examined.

Advertising can be a positive, beneficial force. It can be a flyer for the circus, an encouragement to vote, a declaration of goodwill or a call for funds for a good cause. It can be as simple as a signpost or information as to where something can be found; however . . . there is more to modern advertising than meets the eye. Advertising can be a dark and subversive art. Many times its goal is to pry into the unconscious mind and tinker with the deepest and darkest fears, insecurities and anxieties of the weak. By identifying a weakness, advertising drives a wedge into a splinter of insecurity and magnifies it for the world to see. Like poison, it sinks in the consciousness of its victim and then dangles a remedy to alleviate the pain. It is power to control the hearts and minds of consumers.

This is where advertising, which is really only a tool, like a hammer or a bullhorn, can turn ugly. When advertisers understand the tactics to exploit weakness and sin and are capable of crafting images and impressions that have resonant psychological affects, then we're talking about a force that can have some real impact on society. The implications of channeling such a force are boundless". Basically, the goal of the marketer is to make you feel bad about yourself or your life, then offer up the solution for your poor situation.

I love fishing. It began as an obsession during my youth as it took me away from the confines of boredom into a world of freedom and adventure. I was a true modern-day Tom Sawyer and found a great deal of excitement with a fishing pole. Even as a child I noticed something . . . fish are stupid animals! One summer afternoon while fishing with a buddy, I caught a big ole bass. It was huge, a real whopper! With all my strength I pulled him in but just before I could get my hands on him the line snapped and he flopped back into the water. Unfortunately, he still had my favorite lure stuck in his mouth. Ten minutes later, I had another huge tug on my line and to my bewilderment; I pulled in the same fish. He still had my favorite lure stuck in his mouth. "What an idiot", I thought with boyish wonder.

The point here isn't the fish but rather the nature of the fish. He is always looking for something to eat. He eats smaller fish that appear shiny in water; therefore, he is attracted to shiny things because he doesn't know any better. Unbeknownst to the fish, something more intelligent knows he likes shiny things and creates a trap out of a shiny object, in this case, my lure. The result of his ignorance and inability to tell the difference is the frying pan. That is the unfortunate reality of this situation we call life.

Small children love shiny things, too. They lack the understanding and maturity to make proper decisions and, just like the fish, will always be attracted to the shiny things. Place a $100 bill in one hand and a handful of shiny nickels in the other and offer the child a choice. In most cases, he will choose the shiny nickels because he has no concept of the value of the unattractive $100 bill. He lacks the maturity and the discipline to understand, and that is exactly how advertising works. They are fishing everyday for stupid fish. They dangle lures in front of us constantly and cast their nets into our seas of consumer ignorance. You must understand and avoid their tactics, or you will end up in the debt frying pan. You have to be smarter than the advertisers. You want to be the one who always gets away.

Remember, advertising is simply a method to separate you from your money. Catchy phrases like "New and Improved" are simply new and improved marketing campaigns to get you to purchase. It is a very simple concept, but if you do not verse yourselves in the mindset of those advertisers you will be hooked to their deception before you can realize it. They will always tempt you with stuff you DO NOT NEED. As for me, I will never fall for that fancy loop de loop toy again. As for the ignorant fish, unfortunately he'll never get a second chance to learn from his ignorant mistake. Don't be an ignorant fish. It is imperative that you understand simple marketing lies and deceptions to avoid the advertisers' frying pan.

CHAPTER 3

THE MAKING OF A BEAST MASTER

"If my sons wished for there to be no wars, there would be none" . . . Guttle Rothschild

IN THE EARLY 1700'S, a Jewish goldsmith named Moses Amschel Bauer left the anti-Semitic (anti-Jewish) region of eastern Europe and travelled west into Germany where he settled in the town of Frankfurt. Once there, he set up shop at Frankfurt am Main where he collected and traded gold coins and other valuable items, as he was known as a goldsmith or moneychanger by profession. It was while living in the ghetto called Judengasse (Jew Alley) that his son Mayer Amschel Bauer was born in 1744. As the boy grew, his father had become more and more successful at business, and there would be room for young Amschel to learn and grow in his father's trade.

At a very early age, Mayer Amschel Bauer possessed an immense intellectual ability for dealing with gold and things of monetary value. The prodigy child showed remarkable talent for business as well. His father, over the years, spent a great deal of his time teaching his son everything he could about the money lending business even though the old man originally hoped to have his son trained as a rabbi. The father's untimely death in 1756 changed the course of the boy's future.

Following his father's demise, young Amschel took a job as a clerk in a money lending house owned by the Oppenheim family in Hanover. He worked under the direct supervision of Jacob Wolf Oppenheim who took note of the young man's keen banking talents. His superior ability in banking and uncanny skill at usury was quickly recognized, and his advancement within the firm was swift. In no time, he was awarded a junior partnership at a very young age and began to fill his own accounts with a modest amount of wealth. He soon returned to Frankfurt and purchased the same business that his father had started years earlier. Outside the shop hung a red shield with a gold Roman eagle in the middle which had been placed there by his father in the early years of the business. The red shield symbolized the Jewish struggle for revolution in Eastern Europe. Amschel clearly understood the significance in the meaning of the red shield which in German was pronounced "rot schild." As his family business became more established, it became known generally as the house of the rot schild or, in the English variant, "Rothschild" which he adopted as his family name - a name the entire world would come to know quite well over the next 200 years.

While young Amschel (Bauer) Rothschild was working at the Oppenheimer Bank, he ran errands for a Hessian General named Von Estorff. He reunited his dealings with General Von Estorff as a hopeful avenue for future opportunities. The General was attached to the court of Prince William of Hanau, the House of Hess (Denmark, Norway and the Hessian lands north of Frankfurt) who also had a keen interest in rare coins which Amschel Bauer "Rothschild," like his father, dealt in. By offering coins and other precious metals at discount prices, Rothschild was soon in good graces with the General as well as other influential members of the court, including Prince William himself who also began to purchase coins and work directly with Rothschild. This was Rothschild's first transaction with a head of state which opened his pocketbook to a new found way to wealth.

Soon, he had several transactions with heads of states and a direct route to business with the nobles.

By 1770, Amschel Mayer Rothschild was on his way to a wealthy future when he married 17 year old Guttle Schnaper. They had five sons and five daughters. Their sons would all play a pivotal role in the Rothschild's becoming the wealthiest family on the planet. Amschel taught each of his sons the ins and outs of the banking business, actually, "his" banking business. Once each son was old enough, he was sent to a major European city to set up a Rothschild bank or lending house. His first son Amschel Mayer, the junior, went back and forth from Frankfurt to Berlin, Salomon Mayer to Vienna, Jacob Mayer or James to Paris, Karl Mayer or Kalmann to Naples and Nathan Mayer to London. Soon, the Rothschild's had set up a web of banks that would take over Europe as they became the first international bankers, and the financial world changed forever.

Once in the graces of Prince William, the Rothschild future was financially unlimited. It seems Prince William, whose family had been encapsulated by royalty since the dark ages, was very willing to loan soldiers, for the right price, to any country in current need of a boost to their military forces. His most loyal customer was England, to whom he gladly rented copious amounts of uniformed troops who were used to keep the American colonies from revolting.

Rothschild had become William's financial agent in the rent-a-troop business, according to Des Griffin in his book <u>Descent into Slavery</u>, which would yield him well as William was one of the wealthiest men in all of Europe. When Napoleon's armies forced William of Hess to flee Denmark, he entrusted much of his fortune to Rothschild, a sum worth millions of dollars in our currency today. A portion of this money was actually paid to William by England for the use of troops and was to be forwarded as payment to those troops. Rothschild, however, saw a great opportunity to put the funds to good use by loaning the money as capital for governments during the Napoleonic wars in which he would net incredible wealth in interest.

It was at the time of Napoleon's attempt at world domination when Rothschild dispatched his son Nathan (the lesser) to England to open the family bank in London. He sent with him the sum of three million dollars. According to the Jewish Encyclopedia, 1905, "Nathan then invested the money into gold from the East Indies Company, knowing that it would be needed for Wellington's peninsula campaign. On this, Nathan made no less than four profits; first on the sale of Wellington's paper which he purchased at fifty cents on the dollar then collected the lot, then on the sale of gold to Wellington. Thirdly, he repurchased that very gold at a profit and finally, he forwarded that profit onto the Portuguese government for the same purposes and making further healthy profits. It was this huge opportunity that set the Rothschild's dynasty up in Europe and financially allowed the other four sons banking adventures in their respective cities while setting up their financial headquarters in London."

By the late 1700's, the Rothschild's were on their way to becoming the wealthiest family in the world. By financing governments, they achieved wealth far beyond that of their benefactor, Prince William of Hess. The Rothschild behavior with monetary means was far beyond any business model that had ever been bred up to that time including those of the Knights Templar in France centuries before. With acute cunning and financial wizardry the likes the world had never seen, it was as if Amschel Mayer Rothschild had some kind of vision into the future and could be one step ahead of the game of governmental and military maneuvers with a keen and unfeeling apathy in regards to who got in the way. With five sons in charge of the well designed web, the Rothschild's soon had an intelligence agency that was far superior to that of any government and could acquire and send information throughout their system in matters of days in a time that information took months to travel.

One well known legend of the Rothschild's is the story surrounding the battle of Waterloo which held the future of Europe in its grips. If Napoleon emerged victorious, France would enter the stage as the lone power house. If England defeated Napoleon; they would hold the balance of power and would be in a position to expand their influence upon the world. As the battle ensued, a lone agent of Rothschild's stood poised for the outcome delivered to him by carrier pigeons. Once he was assured by his military connections that Wellington would surely emerge victorious he was whisked away to an awaiting vessel where he travelled by moonlight to England where he was met by Nathan Rothschild himself. That very morning Rothschild, knowing the news of Napoleon's defeat wouldn't reach London for another day, enhanced the family fortune in yet another cold and calculated move.

The Jewish Encyclopedia recalls the day's event as such: "As Rothschild leaned against the pillar at the London Stock Exchange, he hung his heavy hands into his pockets and began to release silent, motionless, impeccable cunning. Those around him began to suspect that he knew something. He began to dump his share of English consuls (English bonds of that time) on the market; naturally those watching took heed and began doing the same. As the day wore on English monetary stock plummeted to an all time low and those attending assumed that Napoleon must have crushed Wellington. Rothschild stood, for some time, emotionless, expressionless and continued to sell, sell, and sell. The selling turned into a panic as people rushed to sell their worthless consuls in exchange for gold and silver in hopes of retaining at least part of their wealth. The consuls dropped to a record five cents on the dollar.

Then, just as emotionless he began to give a different signal. Dozens of agents began making their ways to the order desks around the Exchange and bought up every available consul. A short time later the official news arrived. Wellington had defeated Napoleon and England was now master of Europe as the price of the English consul was suddenly at an all time high and Rothschild owned almost all of it. Nathan Rothschild had bought control of the British economy in one swoop. In one day, June 15, 1815, he had multiplied his family wealth twenty times over."

Then, to add insult to injury, the Rothschild's made another bold and calculated move in France. Following the defeat at Waterloo, the French struggled to regain a financial foothold. In 1817, the French government negotiated a substantial loan from the French banking house of Ouvrard and from the Baring Brothers of London. This move left the controlling Rothschild's out in the cold. The following year, the unstable French were in bad need of another loan. As the bonds issued the prior year were increasing in value on the Paris market, and in other European financial centers, it appeared certain that the French would retain the services of the two distinguished money houses.

All the while, the Rothschild's attempted several maneuvers to advance their interests with the French government to secure their advance into governmental loans but were unsuccessful. The French aristocrats didn't wish to do business with newbie's like the Rothschild's even though the family had secured vast financial resources which the French had overlooked or were basically ignorant of the family's unprecedented cunning in their ability to manipulate money and monarchs.

Then, on November 5, 1818, after a year of appreciation the French government bonds mysteriously began to fall. With each passing day, the decline got worse. Within a short span of time, other government securities began to fall as well. Louis the XVIII began to worry about the financial stability of the country as one adviser after another brought him more and more bad news. The only people around the French court who weren't worried were James and Karl Rothschild who said nothing. Some began to suspect the Rothschild's of somehow manipulating the bond market and creating a panic. And they had.

History reveals that in October of 1818, Rothschild agents, using the family's unlimited reserves, bought huge quantities of French government bonds issued through their rivals Ouvrard and Baring Brothers. This caused the bonds to increase in value. Then, on November 5th, they began to dump the bonds in huge quantities on the open market in the main commercial centers of Europe, throwing the French market into a panic. The Rothschild's had now gained the financial control of France as well as England, and the world was theirs.

Unfortunately, Mayer Amschel Rothschild, the architect of the most financially powerful family in the world, died on September 19, 1812, and did not live to see the complete takeover of the European financial market by his sons. He did, however leave a will that kept his vision alive for two more centuries. As documented by Des Griffen, in <u>Descent into Slavery</u>, in the will he laid down very specific rules to be followed to the letter by his descendants, both living and those yet to be born. The rules were to be followed accordingly and anyone who attempted to stray from them would be expelled.

(a) All key positions in the House of Rothschild were to be held by members of the family and never by hired hands. Only male members of the family were ever to be allowed to participate in business. The eldest son of the eldest son was to be the head of the family unless the majority of the rest of the family agreed otherwise. It was for this exceptional reason that Nathan, who was particularly brilliant, was appointed head of the House of Rothschild in 1812.

(b) The family was to intermarry with their own first and second cousins, thus preserving the vast fortune. (This rule was strictly adhered to early on but later, when other rich Jewish banking houses came on the scene, it was relaxed to allow some of the Rothschild's to marry selected members of the new elite).

(c) Amschel forbid his heirs *"most explicitly, in any circumstances whatever, to have any public inventory made by the courts, or otherwise, of my estate . . . Also, I forbid any legal action and any publication of the value of the inheritance . . . Anyone who disregards these provisions and takes any kind of action which conflicts with them will immediately be regarded as having disputed the Will, and will suffer the consequences of so doing."*

(d) Rothschild ordered a perpetual family partnership and provided that for the female members of the family, their husbands and children should receive their interest in the estate subject to the management of the male members. They were to have no part in the management of the business. Anyone who disputed this arrangement would lose their interest in the Estate.

The House of Rothschild was based on several important factors. The first being complete secrecy resulting from total control of all business arrangements and dealings along with an uncanny and almost supernatural ability to see what lie ahead and take full advantage of all monetary situations. The whole family seemed to be driven by an insatiable lust for the accumulation of wealth and power with total ruthlessness and unsympathetic dealings in all business matters.

By the early part of the 19th century, the Rothschild family had clearly taken over Europe and the beast of International Banking had been born and would lay the foundations of the modern banking system of perpetual debt upon the world through the process of usury. The monetary control this one family now had over the populace was extremely dangerous and would affect every human being in one manner or another over the next 200 years. The Rothschild's had discovered that there existed the potential of untold wealth and power in controlling the finances of nations and never before in the history of the world had one government or organization ever done so, let alone one family. The beast would soon be out of its cage.

"Allow me to control the wealth of a nation and I care not who makes its laws" . . . *Nathan Amschel Rothschild.*

The family had grown incredibly powerful by financing governments and wars, and all five Rothschild brothers were equal in their collective understanding of cunning and conquest in their web system of international banking. The family didn't seem to rely on any true friendships outside the estate as everyone was considered tools for business or they had no use. Everyone seemed to be a stepping stone for financial gain and untold power that would manipulate governments, armies and the general population for a long time to come.

Frederick Morton, author of the The Rothschild's: A Biography, states, *"In 1806, Napoleon declared that it was his objective to remove the house of Hess-Cassel from the ruler ship and to strike it out of the list of powers, thus Europe's mightiest man decreed erasure of the rock on which the new Rothschild firm had been built. Yet, curiously, the bustle didn't diminish at the house of the Red Shield . . . Rothschild still sat, avid and impenetrable, portfolios wedged between body and arm.*

They saw neither peace nor war, neither slogans or manifestos, nor orders of the day, neither death nor glory. They saw none of the things that blinded the world. They saw only steppingstones. Prince William had been one, Napoleon another."

Some historians claim the Rothschild's were financing the British and Napoleon both and as a result, the House of Rothschild had free access to French financial markets as well as English during the wars. And all that money that the Rothschild bank hid for Prince William was returned in whole once the former was able to return home. The money made millions of dollars in interest as the Rothschild's used it to further their wealth. That information, according to historians was kept in the family, and the Prince was none the wiser.

The Rothschild's families began to expand into all of Europe by the mid to late 19th Century. Five lines of the Austrian branch of the family were elevated in Austrian nobility, being given hereditary baronies of the Habsburg Empire by Emperor Francis II in 1816. The British branch was elevated into nobility by Queen Victoria. In doing so, the family had a foothold in governmental policy-making as well with world-wide banking influence through English domination and world colonization through the Crown's East India Company.

The family was not only making millions financing the industrial revolution but was also financing entire countries. In 1811, Nathan Mayer Rothschild established his London business at New Court in St. Swithin's Lane, where it still operates today. In 1818, he arranged a 5 million pound loan to the Prussian government, and the issuing of bonds for government loans formed a mainstay of his business. He gained a position of such power in the city of London that by 1825, he was able to supply the Bank of England to enable it to avert a market liquidity crisis.

The family business pioneered international high finance across the globe. They financed industrialization and the expansion of the railroad systems across all of Europe and into America during the industrial age in the late 1800's. Most people believed that John D. Rockefeller was the wealthiest man in the world. Upon his death, it was discovered that the Rothschild's actually owned 71 percent of his holdings. They financed the Japanese government during the Russo-Japanese War by the issuance of Japanese War bonds totaling approximately 11.5 million pounds. They financed the building of mining companies, oil companies, wineries and hundreds of other adventures worldwide.

But a challenge was on the horizon for the family. By the late 1700's a new country had been born, one created like none other in which individual liberties and state's rights would insure opportunity to the populace in a method that would not require money lending on the scale that it did in Europe. This was a threat to the Rothschild's, especially if that idea could spread into Europe, not to mention the fact that untold fortunes would be had for the banking system that could take America the way that it took Europe.

America was unique in modern history. It was only the second nation in history to have ever been formed with the Holy Bible as its law book. Its uniquely magnificent Constitution was specifically designed to limit the power of government and to keep its citizens free and prosperous through the foundation of a Republic. Its citizens were basically industrious immigrants who yearned to be free and who asked nothing more than to be given the opportunity to live and work in such a wonderfully stimulating environment that offered opportunity to anyone willing to take the risks that freedom demanded. America was viewed by the world as the new promise land.

The big bankers in Europe viewed the wonderful results borne by this unique experiment from an entirely different perspective; as a major threat to their future plans. Frederick Morton quotes the establishment Times of London: *"If that mischievous financial policy which had its origin in the North American Republic (Constitutionally authorized no debt money) should become indurate down to a fixture, then that government will furnish its own money without cost. It will pay off its debts and be without a debt, it will become prosperous beyond precedent in the history of civilized governments of the world. The brains and wealth of all countries will go to North America. That government must be destroyed or it will destroy every monarchy on the globe."*

It was suspected by some historians that the Rothschild's financed the failed second British invasion of 1812 and their known first financial move into the affairs of the United States came in the 1820s and 30s when the family, via their agent Nicholas Biddle, fought to defeat Andrew Jackson's move to curtail the international bankers. The bankers lost the first round when in 1832, President Jackson vetoed the move to renew the charter of the Bank of the United States (a central bank controlled by international bankers) thereby paying off the national deficit in full resulting in a debt free nation. In 1836, the bank was forced to close its doors.

*"You are a den of thieves and vipers, and I intend to rout
you out, and by the Eternal God, I will rout you out."*
President Andrew Jackson, 1836

Some historians and most conspiracy theorists speculate that
the Rothschild's and their agents were instrumental in influencing
the rebellion of the southern states which resulted in the American
Civil War. When Abraham Lincoln searched for banks to finance
the Union during the war, the international bankers were more
than happy to oblige with interest rates of 32 to 36 percent. Lincoln
stated, *"I have Bobby Lee and the Southern Army in front of me and the
banks in back of me, of the two foes, it is the one at my rear that is my
true enemy."* In December 1861, large numbers of European troops
(British, French and Spanish) poured into Mexico in defiance of
the Monroe Doctrine. This, with European aid to the Confederacy,
strongly indicated that the Crown was preparing to enter the war,
if and when it looked financially feasible for certain investors to
do so.

Lincoln appealed to Russia for assistance and Czar Alexander II,
who had his own misadventures with the house of the red shield, was
more than happy to send help. On September 24, 1863, a Russian
fleet under command of Admiral Liviski, steamed into New York
harbor and anchored there. Another Russian fleet under Admiral
Popov arrived in San Francisco on October 12.

History reveals that the European bankers were heavily involved
in financing both sides in the Civil War. Lincoln, however, put a
stop to that when he refused to pay the outrageous interest rates.
Lincoln re-established a government backed bond to create our own
monies that would no longer require the services of international
bankers. The Rothschild's venture to bring international banking
into American government had failed again, but they would not give
up there. Biding their time, they knew at some point the opportunity
to get their foot into the door of the government of the United

States would someday present itself. We will cover that in the next chapter.

> *"The division of the United States into two federations of equal force was decided long before the civil war by the high financial power of Europe. These bankers were afraid that the United States, if they remained in one block and as one nation, would attain economical and financial independence, which would upset their financial domination over the world.*
>
> *The voice of the Rothschild's predominated. They foresaw the tremendous booty if they could substitute two feeble democracies, indebted to the financiers, to the vigorous Republic, confident and self-providing.*
>
> *Therefore they started their emissaries in order to exploit the question of slavery and thus dig an abyss between the two parts of the Republic."* Otto Von Bismarck, 1876

After amassing huge fortunes, the very name of Rothschild had become synonymous with extravagance and great wealth, and the family was renowned for its art collecting, its palaces and its philanthropy. By the end of the 19th century, the family owned or had built, at the lowest estimates, over 41 palaces across Europe, of a scale and luxury perhaps unparalleled even by the wealthiest royal families. The Rothschild's banking business was behind most self-made millionaires of the day. Even in America, names like Rockefeller, Carnegie and Vanderbilt depended on the Rothschild's for leverage as they built their personal empires throughout the United States.

Most self made millionaires over the course of history lost their fortunes through heredity as their heirs usually squandered it over two or three generations. But not the House of Rothschild. They are as powerful and wealthy today as they were two hundred years ago.

Amschel Mayer Rothschild would be very proud knowing how his family respected his desire to create a dynasty and though there are now hundreds of descendents living in various countries, a sense of loyalty to the family business still keeps them connected, and their political and financial influence in the world remains as strong as ever.

Since the end of the 19th century, the family has taken a low-key public profile, donating many of their most famous estates, as well as vast quantities of art, to charity, keeping full anonymity about the size of their fortunes and avoiding conspicuous displays of wealth.

Today the Rothschild's and their descendents are well invested in literally thousands of industries, organizations and banking businesses worldwide as well as geo-political and world government entities. It is reported by some researchers that the family wealth now runs in the trillions of dollars, more than the entire wealth of some nations. The Rothschild's recently moved capital assets and other acquisitions in the food and agribusiness sectors in order to help their Continuation Holdings AG to gain a wider capitol pool which would enlarge its presence in the Asian market as well. Their London Investment Bank, NM Rothschild and Sons, does most of its business and acquisitions advisors with untold capital expenditures and continuing profits in the billions of dollars. In France, the Rothschild's own or are heavily invested in almost all the large wineries and various high tech and other industries. Their banks in that country include, amongst others, Compagnie Financie're Edmond de Rothschild and Banque privee Edmond de Rothschild, La Compagne Benjamin de Rothschild S.A. and COGIFRANCE and the list goes on.

So what does any of this have to do with you? Well, a great deal. A glimpse into the vast powers of one family with untold wealth can give each individual a keen insight into the workings of our current geo-political and financial situation. This is an integral part of your learning process, and I have spent a considerable amount of time on this chapter because you must understand the workings of this system in high places. The rich and powerful have manipulated governments and policy makers for centuries, and no single unit has done so with such cold, calculated cunning as the House of Rothschild and their benefactors. They seem to have investments in every monetary system throughout the world, and their manipulation of those systems can have an extreme adverse affect on the very lives of each and every citizen of those countries, including the United States. The truth is, the Rothschild's are the International Banking System and as we will see, this system, designed 250 years ago by Amschel Mayer Rothschild has come to full fruition by encapsulating a world of bondage for the average US citizen who thought he was free of such tyrants only to find that the plastic purchasing power in his wallet was actually his ball and chain.

I am saying that those who have obscene wealth tend to manipulate, intimidate and influence governments and institutions directly or indirectly which will have an enormous affect on everyone in the United States, including you. The history of the Rothschild family is an excellent example of how the very wealthy at the top can manipulate the masses through influencing governmental policy and law makers in order to increase banking and business profits. America has had its giants such as John Rockefeller, J.P. Morgan, and Andrew Carnegie just to name a few, but none of them have been able to manipulate policy or markets worldwide the way the Rothschild's have and truth be known, those very giants have been known to deal directly with the House of Rothschild in one venture or another. The Rothschild's, and those just like them, unlike "Pinky and the Brain" are not necessarily hatching a plot to take over the world, but they are hatching plots daily designed to increase their wealth and power over systems and peoples . . . which includes you. And they do it by understanding the very nature of mankind.

While we were sleeping and consuming, master minds of unscrupulous venture coupled with the lust of wealth and power were in constant thought of designing systems that would add to their coffers by manipulating the masses to purchase product through the means of constant and perpetual debt. By understanding and taking full advantage of our own selfish nature, this system, this beast, would seem to be mastered by entities far more cunning and ruthless than mere mortal men. You are but a stepping stone in that venture, and your only defense is knowledge with the ability to act upon that knowledge less we all become slaves to the "powers and principalities in high places" ready to enslave us all.

But these *"powers that be"* know that the masses will not rise up as long as they can partake in the scraps from the tables of the banksters who will provide the physical comforts that the middle class demand. Like a bird in a cage, we are none the wiser as the rich get richer and the middle class slowly fade away into the coffers of the wealthy.

Middle class Americans have become passive and weak over the last 100 years. Once the industrious muscle of this great republic we have become clay in the hands of high corporate finance, easily molded and controlled by those who use our misfortune and financial ignorance as pawns in their game of international finance and monetary slavery.

Perhaps your only tool is awareness that your biggest enemy is yourself. Our only hope in avoiding enslavement by this system is to be debt free. By being debt free, we can avoid their power over our lives and decisions. We must learn to say no to the temptations of materialism. The less we need, the less their power over us and the end result is real freedom. Their best tool is our desire to purchase stuff we cannot afford.

CHAPTER 4

THE BEAST

"Some of the biggest men in the world in the fields of commerce and manufacturing are afraid of something. They know that there is a power somewhere so organized, so subtle, so watchful, so interlocked, so complete, so pervasive, that they had better not speak above their breath when they speak of condemnation of it" . . . *President Woodrow Wilson*

WE HAVE OBVIOUSLY ESTABLISHED the understanding that the average American is completely ignorant of the basic financial system that exists around him and is in constant wonder about where his money goes, or worse has a total disregard for any of it resulting in the marriage of ignorance and apathy because, as long as he can make his monthly payments for his constant comforts, nothing else matters. Perhaps nuclear war could erupt in Europe tomorrow and many Americans would care less as long as it doesn't interrupt their daily routine of working and spending and being entertained. This is exactly what the banking empire is counting on. A collective apathy of social masses creates a country of sheep.

"It is enough that the people of the nation do not understand our banking and monetary system, for if they did, I believe

there would be revolution before tomorrow morning."
–Henry Ford

Most of us find finance a very boring or intimidating subject and will avoid it at all cost. Unfortunately, it is this avoidance that has created ignorance in the very thing that is placing so many good people into debt without their knowledge of the catalyst that is making their lives miserable.

Ignorance and apathy are a married couple who have a mess of kids named Unaware, Idunno, Who cares, What's-in-it-for-me, Gotta have it, and How much is the monthly payment. It is extremely important for those of you who wish to be free of this beastly system to understand the basics of how money works, or you will become a slave to it. There are neither sidelines nor any fence to ride. You're in the game, like it or not. That is our reality. Larry Burkett, author of How to Manage Your Money, said, *"Money makes a wonderful slave but a terrible master."* What a remarkable statement and one that is very fitting. If you do not understand the basics of economy, finances, and perpetual debt, you will live a life of constant worry and dread where money is concerned. It will own you, and you will never have enough as you live a life of consumption with very little production and will be at the whim of those who do understand money quite well.

Know this! Money never sleeps. Money is fluid and is in constant growth. Like two rabbits. Put a boy rabbit and a girl rabbit in the same cage and in a year's time you will have a lot of rabbits. Money works just like rabbits. The offspring of money is called interest and that is what money, in our culture, is all about. Your money will always make more money. If you are in debt, it will always make more money for someone else. If you are not in debt it will always make money for you. The banks know this very simple fact very well. The average person, however, is completely ignorant of it. Because of this simple fact, the world is designed to take your money, mostly via interest on what you borrow, i.e., the house payment, the car payment, the credit cards, etc. For this reason, nothing, and I mean absolutely nothing, beats debt free.

Debt in our culture has become a way of business. Recently, another large airline has declared bankruptcy which will allow it protection from its debtors. This does not mean a company is going out of business the way it use to, rather it simply means a re-organization within so it can start all over without paying its bills. This is called corporate "debt restructuring" which is a fancy name for poor stewardship of fiscal responsibilities on a big scale. Today's corporate business model has this idea that if a company isn't in debt, they aren't taking advantage of growth opportunities. The banking business today advises corporations and businesses to maximize their debts with reasonable risks and calls it "leveraging one's equity".

In the latter part of the 1860's, a man by the name of J.R. Couts drove several hundred head of cattle 1500 miles from Weatherford, Texas, westward through hostile Comanche territories then northwest to Denver and across the Great Divide onward to California. Once there he sold the herd and paid off his ranch hands, sending them back to Texas. He then, very methodically carried $50,000 in his saddle bags back home via Denver, to Little Rock, down to New Orleans, back over to Houston then back north to Weatherford in an attempt to avoid any bush-whacking scoundrels or hostile Comanche who might lay in wait for his well known pocket book (or scalp). Once back in Weatherford, which was a pioneer village at the time, he found no secure location to keep his new found wealth and Weatherford had no bank. So, being the industrious sort, he purchased a prime corner lot just north of the county court house in the center of town and built a huge safe there. He then placed a building around it. Soon, others were asking if they could keep their valuables in the bank and suddenly, JR Couts who was a known cattleman and owner of fine race horses was now a banker as he established Citizens National Bank which operated for over 100 years as a local business. That bank still exists today but is now owned by a much larger chain, and of course the methodology used by J.R. Couts is by no means how banking is done in America today.

The first lesson in understanding how money works is by understanding the basic principles of modern banking, so here is a lesson in banking 101 as taught from the perspective of a regular guy. Most people think that banks are institutions of our deposits of savings. In other words, we deposit our money in the bank (like J.R. Couts, cowboy-banker-extraordinaire), and they use that money to loan out to other people and businesses in order to collect a reasonable and honest amount of interest. Therefore, making a profit and everybody is happy. Well, that is only a tiny bit of what the banks are actually about, especially big banks. They are definitely about making money but not in the way most people understand.

The current US economy is all about debt. Debt is big business, and the banks are all about it. When I was a child, there were three locally owned banks in my hometown of about 14,000 people. Today our town has a population of about 26,000 people but now has 16 banks and several quick cash establishments (at least until this debt problem catches up with us), and most are owned by large banks from somewhere else. Why? Because, most Americans are deep in debt! Bankers are debt salesmen, and debt is what modern banking is all about. Perpetual debt is the structure of modern banking, and it is making big banks filthy rich. The numerous amount of banks in each town today is simply a reflection of our debt culture.

It works like this. Let's say you need a loan to buy your first home. The home will be sold to you for $100,000. The actual cost to build the home was $70,000 for material and labor and $30,000 for the lot located in a new starter sub-division inside a corporate city limit. So, to secure the loan, you go see a mortgage company or broker, which is another name for a certain kind of banker. He is more than happy to see you as long as you can place the estimated 10 percent down payment on the home and will place the home up as collateral in the event you cannot make the payments. As you sit down with said loan officer, he agrees to loan you the funds and takes out a simple sheet of paper with some fancy borders on it and begins to fill it out. This piece of paper is simply a piece of paper until you sign it at which point it suddenly has value. That piece of paper is now a promissory note saying that you will pay the money back to the bank in the agreed amount of time. So far, everything is fair and on the up-and-up. That is, until the magic show begins. The bank just whipped $100,000 out of thin air to guarantee you the loan. They don't have the $100,000 dollars in that bank just for your specific loan. They only have $10,000 which is all they are required to have on hand by the FDIC (Federal Deposit Insurance Corporation) in order to do business with you regarding your loan. All their money (money made on debt interest) exists in the computer or on the books. They guaranteed your loan with fiat or fractional money (a negotiable instrument), money that doesn't really exist but you have to pay this money back with interest. This is usury. They are the only entity allowed to do business this way.

So, you now have $100,000 for the house. But wait, it isn't exactly a $100,000 loan any longer. It's actually a $203,000 loan once the interest (this is what the bank believes is a fair charge for the risk they take) is added, and the principle and interest along with any closing costs, associated fees and points are figured in, to be paid back over a period of thirty years which is the typical period on most fixed home mortgage loans.

So, the banker took a fancy sheet of paper that was worth about 56 cents and gave it a $203,000 value out of thin air. You, on the other hand, cannot pay him back with money created from nothing. You do not qualify to use fiat money to pay back the loan of fiat money. You have to pay back $203,000 real dollars over the next thirty years. This will take you approximately one quarter to one third of your life's earnings to complete. Now, add insurance and taxes and the cost is closer to $300,000 for that home. Meanwhile, that same banker will most likely sell your note to another bank which trades in such commodities as debt obligations. And the bank (or mortgage company), will make sure it takes the interest off the top of your loan. In other words, the first several years you pay on the note mostly goes to pay the bank's interest, leaving you with little or no equity in the home for the first seven years. That is why you can deduct that interest on your income taxes each year (because the government feels sorry for you).

So, a house that cost $70,000 to build turned into $203,000 to be paid back to a guy who didn't have the money to loan in the first place or lift a finger to do the actual work. This places the burden of debt onto the back of the homeowner who will pay back 2.3 times the amount of the actual cost to physically build the house over a time span that will keep him in debt for most of his life. This is exactly what all the great American thinkers warned us of if international bankers ever wormed their way into the American way of life. When the mafia did business like this it was known as loan-sharking, and it was illegal.

Easy as pie, right? In theory, yes, and that is basically how it works; however, today's system of modern banking has become so convoluted and confusing to the average person that it is almost impossible to understand all the creative vehicles that Wall Street has invented through the process of banking deregulation so that we can be ripped off and not know it for years. Let me be clear. Hometown and regional banking is and has been essential for progress and the growth of this great country, but big banks on Wall Street and international bankers have been a problem for the average American for a long time. In order to make tons of money from interest they do not want loans paid off. And they love loaning to corporations and governments because it is an unlimited cash cow of continued interest payments.

To consolidate their grip on power over the last few years, the big banksters created very complicated artificial bubbles of debt that will be impossible to pay back. Complex financial instruments such as paper based on paper, credit default swaps, collateralized debt obligations, mortgage backed securities, asset backed securities, structured investment vehicles, auction rate securities, blah, blah, blah, basically means an immense mass of speculative paper bloated in value due to secret instruments like derivatives designed by the big banking system to make themselves rich through extremely risky financial adventures that have created a delusional bubble. And we won't even go into the untold wealth made in all those fees conjured up by the banking gurus at the corporate top.

> *"The modern banking system manufactures money out of nothing. The process is perhaps the most astounding piece of sleight of hand that was ever invented. Banking was conceived in iniquity and born in sin. Bankers own the Earth. Take it away from them, but leave them the power to create money, and with the flick of the pen they will create enough money to buy it back again . . . Take this great power away from them and all great fortunes like mine will disappear, and they ought to disappear, for then this would be a better and happier world to live in. But if you want to continue to be slaves of the banks and pay the cost of your own slavery, then let bankers continue to create money and control credit'."* Sir Joseph Stamp, The Bank of England

Banks create money every day, not on deposits, not on earnings but on the promise the borrower will pay back a loan with interest. There is a constant demand for credit, and the banks know it. This is our new system. A system in that the total of money created equals the total level of debt. The government prints an outrageous amount of money, but that only accounts for about 5 percent of that which is in circulation. The other 95 percent is the promise to pay back the bank in loans. That is debt, and that is our national situation.

But the banking system got too big for its britches, and it all came crashing down in the fall of 08'. It could be that financial oligarchs engineered the current financial situation just as the Rothschild's did 200 years ago. The big banks on Wall Street were de-regulated through the *Gramm, Leach & Bliley Act of 1999 and HR 5660 Commodities & Futures Modernization Act* which created a huge chasm full of wealth for the pickings. These two well intended laws did away with some of the financial firewalls that were constructed to regulate Wall Street in order to protect our nation from another great depression. Unfortunately, with a complete lack of moral restraint Wall Street bankers behaved more like Bourbon Street drunkards during a Mardi-Gras of unlimited capital investing that was a year earlier illegal. With no regard for the consequences, a party of mass proportion took place on the Rue de Wall which, sooner or later, had to end. That party was at the expense of taxpayers, and we will be paying for it for a long time to come. The Federal Government saw no other choice but to bail them out in fear that our entire financial system would collapse and a worldwide domino effect would ensue because of years of banking irresponsibility. Through derivatives, or inflated stock made from nothing, unethical speculation and exaggerated profits made the rich richer by manipulating the markets with these new Wall Street engineered money-making systems that were now un-regulated to do so.

> *"Whoever controls the volume of money in our country is absolute master of all industry and commerce . . . and when you realize that the entire system is very easily controlled, one way or another, by a few powerful men at the top, you will not have to be told how periods of inflation and depression originate."*
> President James Garfield, 1881 (two weeks before he was assassinated)

And if that isn't enough, we find there is a small group of insiders and foreign investors who are purposely creating artificial money growth and volatility through the Federal Reserve Banking System so if things go bad or if they make any mistakes while scheming, they will be able to appeal to their partner, the Federal Government, to bail them out again. This form of slavery on the American people is far more sophisticated today than it was 200 years ago, but the end result is always financial bondage for the working class. Taxes continue to rise as the financial bubbles are bursting, and the big banks may actually be engineering the process. In the current climate, with bail-out money guaranteed, the banks make money on the way up and on the way down as business and families suffer. The banks argue that they are being attacked by the market . . . THEY ARE THE MARKET! Billions of dollars were given to the big banks by the Bush and Obama Administrations and is considered by some experts to be the biggest heist in the history of the world and far exceeds the Rothschild's European antics of 1812.

But where did the money go? A French bank got $10 billion, Deutch Bank of Germany received $12 billion, Barkley's Bank of Britain received $10 billion and various other foreign banks who were derivative partners of A/G, Goldman Sachs received over $50 billion total. This is the largest transfer of wealth in history. Sound familiar? When asked where the money went, Ben Bernanke, Fed Chairman said, "I don't know." Bonuses on Wall Street were up 17% after the bail out. The CEO of Merrill Lynch (the first domino to fall in this mess) according to the Wall Street Journal was able to secure millions of dollars in bonus money for himself and a few of his executives before his company was taken over by Bank of America, even though his firm showed a record loss of over 21 billion dollars in 2008, proving that the best way to rob a bank is to own one. As the American economy is struggling and unemployment has risen to nine and ten percent, big bankers and corporate CEOs continue to advance their worth annually in the biggest separation of the wealth since the industrial age. And nobody went to jail.

Most bonuses in America are believed by corporate bosses necessary and justified as well deserved and expected among the elites of big corporations. Most of these people feel their position, title and work environment are reason enough for their exuberant pay. Most executive bonuses are based on total compensation for the fiscal year, salary, invested stock options, grants, LTIP payouts and perks, stock gains and value realized by exercising stock options and various other terms unknown to the average person. Through this upper-crest mentality of American royalty, we see annual payouts to corporate executives such as $36.4 million to the CEO of Phillip Morris, $104 million to the CEO of Motorola, $49.7 million to the CEO of Walt Disney, $54 million to the CEO of XTO Energy, $59 million to the CEO of Calgene, $48 million to the CEO of Freeport Copper, $30 million to the CEO of Verizon, $39 million to the CEO of Comcast and Merrill Lynch who gave out remarkable sums in performance bonuses. Four people at the top took most, while four more below them took $64 million leaving six others to divide a mere $62 million among themselves. The Merrill Lynch bonuses were done with taxpayer bailout money according to New York Attorney General Andrew Cuomo.

In 2007, just before the crash, the following CEOs who were instrumental in the financial debacle were absorbing unbelievable profits in financial sector companies some of which, were operating with fraudulent or extreme mismanaged principles.

The CEO of Lehman Brothers made $40.1 million as the company went under in '08. The CEO of Goldman Sachs was paid $67.9 million before his company had to be reorganized into a bank holding company. JP Morgan's CEO took home a total package of $39 million before his company had to take a $39 billion TARP rescue. The CEO of Morgan Stanley managed to take $9 million before his company, was taken over by the federal government. Of course, we have already mentioned the pay for the CEO of Merrill Lynch before his company was absorbed by Bank of America. The

CEO of Freddie Mac arranged himself $11.6 million before Uncle Sam took his company, while the CEO of Wachovia managed over $8 million before his company was taken by Wells Fargo. The CEO of Washington Mutual was paid $14.4 million before his company succumbed to a takeover by JP Morgan/Chase, who subsequently crashed. The CEO of CitiGroup took $38 million in salary before his company had to take a $45 billion dollar bailout of taxpayer monies, and the CEO of American Express took $42.7 million in pay before his company had to be bailed out by $3.4 billion in TARP monies.

That is over $270 million in payouts to just ten people in the financial sector of the great American corporate world in just one year. In the United States alone, billions of dollars in corporate profits are paid out to a small sector of elite CEOs annually. Meanwhile, people like you and me live on strict budgets and reap little from the rewards of economic profits. And to add insult to injury, these guys were bailed out using your "over taxed" dollars to do it.

The banksters of Wall Street along with the Federal Reserve Bank have looted the Federal Treasury. President Obama extended a trillion dollar line of credit to Wall Street banks, insurance companies, mortgage companies, credit card companies, and mutual fund companies, but only large financial institutions which allows them to continue the current system of perpetual debt on the general public which knows no better. The Federal Reserve then told US tax payers that it was none of our business what they did with the monies.

The Federal Reserve Bank, created in 1913 during a very controversial move, is a serious problem for the American people and one that deserves some serious speculation. Most people do not know it, but the Federal Reserve Bank is not federal at all, nor is it a reserve of our money. The actual Federal Reserve was real vaults of gold held at Fort Knox, Kentucky, which backed up our dollar, but that was long ago. The Federal Reserve Bank is, more or less, a holding house for international bankers or simply a fractionalized system of big investors. But it has been given the power to decide what our interest rates will be and loans money to be paid back in interest to print our legal tender notes (dollars) and it is printing money like crazy. Each year, the fed loans funds to Uncle Sam to print money with interest to be paid back in the tune of approximately 20 billion dollars annually of your taxes (actually, it is approximately 6.6 percent of our total national budget) to investors through the federal reserve.

Just what is the Federal Reserve Bank? Glad you asked. From the standpoint of a regular guy, it is a concept born out of the Bank of England in 1694 in which a central bank, backed by private investors through a fractionalized or shared system, would print and control the nation's monetary supply. In other words, it is a small group of private citizens investing in a government's money supply with huge returns after interest is made on the money that they loan. Sounds harmless, but this small group of wealthy investors are not going to invest money into something they can't control so they invest with a heavy say so in what happens to that money supply. By doing so, they control the value of that money supply in every aspect. They manipulate policy makers and governments to behave in ways beneficial to their small groups, and the consequences can be devastating to tax payers. This is exactly how the Rothschild's took the world.

As seen in previous chapters, a central bank was originally kept out of the United States successfully until December 1913, when it was voted in. The Federal Reserve Bank is a corporation chartered by Congress which was given an exclusive franchise to create the nation's money. It is also a mechanism in which Congress has been given access to unlimited taxation through inflation without the American people's knowledge that they are being taxed, and lastly it is a mechanism by which the big banks can earn perpetual interest on nothing by loaning money to it.

Who owns the Federal Banking System? It is actually a corporation. It, like all other corporations, has stock certificates. These certificates are held by member banks within the fractionalized system of several banks (a banking cartel, so-to-speak). The banks in the system are independently owned. The stocks, however, do not act as we know stocks. The owners cannot sell them. The larger banks have more stocks than the smaller ones but each bank has one vote. The system is operated actually by the board and its chairman, appointed by the President of the United States. The certificate holders can only vote for members of boards of their own regional banks. Those chairmen and vice chairmen are appointed by the national board. The national board has veto power, and all power is essentially at the national board which is controlled by five individuals headed by the Fed Chairman.

The Federal Reserve Bank is a hybrid of sorts, a half government/ half private company that creates money from nothing. This is called "fiat" or "fractional" money. It's responsible for stabilizing the economy, to prevent inflation, and protect the general citizenry; however, since its inception in 1913, it has created a system that has seriously inflated the dollar so it can make huge amounts of interest paid on loaning monies via investors on those inflated dollars and it did away with the gold and silver standards so it could not have a limit on how much money could be printed. It has observed corporate debt, outrageous personal debt on the citizens of the United States, out of control bankruptcy statistics, outrageous amounts of money being printed out of thin air, a large portion of our country bought up by foreigners and the top ten percent, and now a major recession and who knows what in the future.

They have managed to make money for their members and secure their place in the market, regulate and reduce the growth of new banks in other parts of the nation by keeping the power mostly in New York. They have destroyed the gold standard to lower interest rates to attract corporations and industry to borrow money from the large banks and pass on any losses to the people to protect the banking system. And, unbeknownst to most Americans, this system didn't just develop over night. It was designed long ago by the heavies involved in international banking who influenced proper officials in Washington to, once again, allow a Central Banking System into the United States (see chapter three). Once they were successful in ridding themselves of the gold and silver standards, then they could place untold value on the dollar in order to inflate it to unbelievable proportions resulting in untold profits for the top dogs via interest made on fiat monies loaned to print those dollars.

Our forefathers fought long and hard to keep the banking interest out of the United States as they believed their interference within the new American system would, once again, create the same oppressive systems that Europe had endured for centuries under the hands of international bankers resulting in the separation of classes. Alexander Hamilton was a strong proponent of the old English banking systems and was at constant odds with many of his peers, especially Thomas Jefferson who strongly opposed the banking system. Jefferson knew what would happen if a federal bank would ever set up shop in America and gave several warnings to future Americans against such an idea. Unfortunately, greed at the top of our government failed to understand his apocalyptic warnings. Jefferson's agrarian ideology lived on through the fabric of time long after his death but began to erode significantly once the banksters began their onslaught into our financial systems after the reconstruction era of the 1870's.

In his book, The Creature from Jekyll Island, writer and researcher, G. Edward Griffen gives a chilling historical account of how it happened and who was involved. If you've been paying attention, you will begin to see some similarities with the powers that be in the last century designing our current Federal Reserve System.

The American industrial revolution after reconstruction brought untold wealth to many banking industrialists such Carnegie, Rockefeller, etc., all financially floated by JP Morgan who was a suspected agent of the Rothschild's banking empire. Many of these men leveraged much of their wealth through European investors such as the Rothschild's as more and more Americans were moving from agrarian lifestyles of farming and independence into more urban surroundings in order to establish better guaranteed earnings for survival than the farm life could offer. Vast changes in the American way of life were just beginning which created huge profits for the big banks on Wall Street as they became more powerful than ever anticipated.

Jekyll Island was an exclusive vacation resort for the very rich located on the shores of Georgia. In 1910, a very secret meeting was arranged there that would lay the groundwork for the Federal Reserve Bank. The meeting had to be very secret because if word of it got out, its design would have been stopped cold by the American people and members of Congress.

Senator Nelson Aldridge, Republican from Rhode Island, was Chairman of the National Monetary System to reform the banking industry. At that time, American voters were very concerned with all the money trust that had become common on Wall Street. The American Industrial Revolution had created a slew of very wealthy people who began to make policy and influence politicians for their own self purposes. One of President Wilson's campaign promises was to help break the money trust over the financial markets of America, and Aldridge was appointed to do just that. Aldridge, however, was a business associate of J.P. Morgan and father-in-law to John D. Rockefeller Jr., so I trust you can see where this is going. Jesse James would have been more trustworthy to serve the American people.

There were six men secretly invited to the meeting with the Senator, each given specific instructions as not to tell anyone where they were going or when they would return, and each was even given a specific code name to use during any transaction between the other six members and Senator Aldridge. These seven men represented approximately one fourth of the entire wealth of the world. They were Senator Nelson Aldridge, Nathan Fiat Andrew, Assistant

Secretary of the US Treasury who later became a Congressman and well-known in the banking circles; Frank Vanderlipp, President of the National City Bank of New York which was the largest and most powerful of all the banks in the country; Henry Davidson Sr., Partner of the JP Morgan Company, one of the largest financial firms in the United States; Charles Norton, President of the First National Bank of New York; Benjamin Strong, head of JP Morgan Bankers Trust Company who would become the first Federal Reserve Chairman; and lastly, Paul Warburg of Germany, the most influential of the group, a partner of Coon & Loeb Company and a representative of, none other than, the Rothschild banking dynasty. At the time, he was one of the single wealthiest men in the world. (Note: the Schiff family who owned Coon & Loeb, along with the Warburg's and Rothschild's were all intermarried and had been for some time).

The politicians were supposed to break up the money trust but, thanks to Aldridge, it was the money trust who instead designed the Federal Reserve Bank, an idea Aldridge believed would create efficiency in our federal financial system. The fox was designing the henhouse again. Had that fact been known, and it wasn't until 1937 when one of the members leaked the truth of the meeting in his memoirs, Congress would have never passed the bill. Up until that point, America had adhered to a free enterprise system whose great success was the result of millions of small businesses, farms, factories, etc., but the new system was a cartel and monopoly designed to rid itself of any competition which would force Americans to borrow money from the banking industry thus making untold riches upon the interest made from those loans. Basically, a handful of fat cats designed a banking cartel to enhance the profit structures of its members as the Federal Reserve and went into partnership with the US government just like the Rothschild's had done in Europe. Aldridge was a heavy-hitter with huge financial aspirations for himself and his associates, like the Rothschild's, his schemes for self would eventually cost the general population dearly.

> *"The Act establishes the most gigantic trust on earth. When the President signs this Bill, the invisible government of the monetary power will be legalized . . . The greatest crime of the ages is perpetrated by this banking and currency bill."*
> Congressman, Charles Lindbergh, 1913

In ten days, seven men secretly created a system that would finally assure big banks a direct highway into the treasury of the United States of America and develop a beastly design of perpetual debt on the citizens of the United States, and on December 23, 1913, while most of the Senate was away for the Christmas break, in the wee hours of the morning, the bill for the creation of the Federal Reserve Bank became law. What that means today is this. The US government spends a lot more than it takes in from taxes, so the Treasury department says, "Hey, we need some money to pay the bills!" So, they say, "We'll just borrow it!" They then print up a mess of bonds (IOU's). Most think bonds are the best and most secure investment because they are backed up by the US government who says they will pay you back by taxing you to do it, but, once again, I digress. Then they call up the Fed and say, "We need some more money", and the Fed (the Federal Reserve Bank) says, "No problemo," and is more than happy to loan the dollars with lots of interest to be paid back to the banksters (who loan the money) to the tune of 20 billion dollars a year.

Where does the Federal Reserve Bank get the money? There is none. It doesn't exist, just like the bank who loaned you the money for your house. It was created out of thin air but, just like your home loan, it has to be paid back in real dollars (taxes) which means you pay it back with interest to international bankers who loaned the money in the first place. The current administration is printing tons of money out of thin air, and the only thing backing it up is a promise to repay the loan. But the bankers don't want the loan paid off. They want it perpetually paid on assuring them a constant flow of your tax dollars via interest annually.

The investment bankers behind the Federal Reserve Bank are taking you, the tax payer, literally, to the bank. The Rothschild's are alive and well in America and after two strikes they hit a home run when they finally succeeded in setting up shop in the US government on a cold winter's night in 1913. And, amazingly, that same year, congress passed the first federal income tax law. What a coincidence!

So, if the Federal Reserve Bank keeps printing money out of thin air, what are the consequences? Glad you asked. It is called inflation. As the Federal Reserve continues its attempt to manipulate our economic system through designed vehicles, it has to keep printing more and more money. This in turn weakens the dollar and creates higher prices on the market for basic goods and services. The fear most experts agree on is this process may create a system of hyper-inflation based on many different factors that could go wrong because of vulnerability. This would have a very serious effect on the price of basic commodities such as food, transportation and everyday household goods. This in turn could have very serious social and economic consequences.

Currently, the national debt has hit an all time high of approximately 14.3 trillion dollars, and the US government continues to print more and more money backed by the Federal Reserve Bank who loans that money to be paid back with interest through the taxation of American citizens to wealthy financial investors. The Federal Reserve controls the interest rate and our money supply and has never been audited and as Ben Bernanke, the Chairman of the Federal Reserve says, "Never will be." It answers to no one and is accountable to no one. The beast is alive and well in Washington DC.

> *"I believe that banking institutions are more dangerous*
> *than standing armies . . . If the American people ever*
> *allow private banks to control the currency . . . the banks*
> *and the corporations that grow up around them will deprive*

> *the people of their property until their children wake up homeless on the continent their fathers conquered."* Thomas Jefferson

The Federal Reserve Bank determines the value of the dollar. The only thing that gives our money value is how much is in circulation, and the Federal Reserve Bank does that, too. Those with the power to determine a nation's money supply also have the power to regulate its value and therefore, has the power to bring a nation to its knees. So, who are these investors behind the Fed? Most likely, many of the same people who were running other organizations such as Lehman Brothers, AIG, Sachs and JP Morgan.

These are worldly investors who do not have the same mindset or guided by the same conscious as the everyday working man. They are definitely not regular guys. They are not about making monthly payments, worrying about healthcare or how to pay the bills. They are not concerned with the problems of your community. They could care less about your problems, the problems of the sick, poor, or the displaced. They are only concerned with making money and not just money as we understand it, but unholy profits, and they will make it on the way up by unscrupulous schemes designed to pull in untold wealth via interest on the dollar or on the way down through outrageous bonuses created from your taxes. And they will feel very justified in doing so as they pat themselves on the back via your ignorance of current monetary systems.

The biggest problem with the Federal Reserve is that they are risking our very way of life by continuing to print money leveraged by countries such as Japan, China and India who are frankly tired of bankrolling our spending habits. Municipalities are broke, state governments are broke and the federal government is broke, yet it refuses to admit it. If China called in the loans tomorrow, the result could be hyper-inflation as the dollar collapses. The US dollar has been the world reserve currency since WWII. Before then, the British Pound Sterling was the world reserve currency for almost 200 years until England had to be bailed out by the US after the war. The dollar then took the world stage and America flourished. The fact is several world countries are now looking for other options than the over-leveraged dollar because of the American debt problem caused by our current banking system and our continued spending.

Some may argue that it makes no sense for the big banks to cause the collapse of the American financial system as it would mean a loss of their bread and butter. Wrong! Like a virus, the international banking system is simply using America as a host. If the American financial system were to collapse the bankers would just find another host and right now, the Chinese and Asian systems are looking pretty tastey and major worldly investors are beginning to shift investments toward that market. Thanks to companies such as Wal-Mart and US consumption, China is becoming the world superpower.

Usury is a system condemned by every major religion because it is a process that makes interest on fiat monies, basically money made out of nothing which in turn places huge burdens on a society while disguised as a higher standard of living for all. In today's market, as in the example I showed earlier of the cost of the house and how it is financed, producers get very little and the banks, through the process of usury, are creating inflated profits through debt interest created out of nothing.

The beast is subduing the general population into bondage and a life of perpetual debt that will be impossible to rise above and just like the serfs of the middle-ages; we are paying our daily bread to the overlords. The middle class is deteriorating into the pits of leverage. Basically, if things don't change, the banking system will indirectly control everyone through purchase and influence and no one will be able to compete in business, buy, sell or even eat without using them at a profit to do so.

"And that no man might buy or sell, save he that had the mark, or the name of the beast, or the number of his name."
The book of Revelation

Meanwhile, local, state and federal governments will begin to cut budgets as mislead protestors will blame capitalism and elected officials on the left, the right and in the middle, all the while never understanding who the real enemy is. So now you have a better idea how the modern banking system works and how it directly affects you and your family. So what can you do about it? Read on.

CHAPTER 5

My Money Has Wings

"Discipline is the closest to God we'll ever be on this planet." - M. Scott Peck

THE LATE LARRY BURKETT, writer of several financial books, was quoted as saying, *"Managing money is only 20 percent math and 80 percent behavior."* We will pay the price of discipline or the price of the consequences of not having it. In my earlier days, I found myself in the unfortunate circumstances of a divorced man, left with a house, a mortgage, all the bills, and a baby with no child support. Over the next two years my lack of wealth in financial knowledge would lead me into the world of the average American . . . deep in dept with no way out. I could barely pay my bills. I even went so far as to remove light bulbs around the mirrors in the bathrooms in hopes of saving on the utility bills, and I lived in constant terror of the car breaking down. Each morning I woke with a financial hangover of Biblical proportions. I soon found myself with two maxed-out credit cards, and the credit card companies wouldn't give me the time of day when I attempted to "work out a payment plan." Each month I was tagged with late fees and extreme high interest rates. My life was a financial mess.

My situation was not created by my ex-wife, nor was it created by my lack of a better paying job so much as it was created by my complete and utter ignorance of personal finances and the banking system. Never had anyone, including my high school or college education ever explained the real financial system in America or how it worked. I had classes in high school that taught me how to write checks and balance a checkbook and I had basic macro and micro economics in college, but nobody prepared me for the real world of debt finances. After all, I came from generational poorness and thought I was just doing what I was supposed to do.

It was on a Friday afternoon in 1996 when my eyes were opened to the truth. My employer at that time was a wonderful middle-aged woman who truly cared for her staff. I met with her that very day to ask for a raise, which she denied. Instead she gave me a gift that would change my generational ignorance of money management forever. She introduced me to a person who had a whole different take on money. He was living totally debt free and explained to me the truth about the American financial system and how it was turning me into a slave to monthly payments. That was my revelation and the day my life changed.

The idea of debt free was foreign to me, but it didn't take long before I would accept this new philosophy of controlling my spending and paying off debt as I realized an entirely radical way of thinking about money. At first I thought the way out of debt was something I could not afford because I lived so frugally, but once I began to put a few of my newly learned philosophical views into practice, life began to change . . . radically. Why? Because I finally discovered the key to changing my financial situation lay in changing my financial behavior.

I soon began to understand that the "American Dream" was a big fat lie . . . sold to me by banks, financial institutions and advertising. I had always been told that the American dream was life, liberty and the pursuit of happiness . . . mostly, my self-serving happiness.

No one had ever told me the truth about finances before. I was finally delivered from the indoctrination of my ignorant financial upbringing of spending and debt and washed in the blood of truth.

I stopped spending money on non-essential items. I traded my "manly" SUV in for a used Honda Civic that got 32 mpg. I got rid of all my credit cards by paying them off then cutting them up. I got a new credit card with a $500 limit so I couldn't overspend. I stopped using my credit card for mostly everything and forced the two card companies that I owed to work with me to pay off those maxed out cards. I stopped eating out and renting movies until I got a handle on my finances. I worked with other creditors to set up payment plans on outstanding debt and found all of them agreeable to work with me to pay off those bills. I used Dave Ramsey's debt snowball plan to pay them off starting with the smallest first and working my way up until I was caught up. Before I knew it, I had paid off my outstanding debt in half the time I expected. The only bills left were the car payments and the house. I found my biggest enemy to be me and my lack of discipline and desire to impersonate an image of what the world told me I needed to keep up. Once I accepted my own denial about my spending habits and took personal responsibility for my situation, everything changed overnight. To borrow from Dr. Martin Luther King, "Free at last! Free at last! Thank God almighty, I am free at last!" It can be done.

The banks and the corporate industrial complex had taught me well how to be a slave. Once I began to understand their deception of financial logic and mass advertising, I began to understand freedom in a whole new way. By understanding their tactics, you can beat them at their own game if you are willing to change the way you think about money, the world around you and your place in it. However, a stern warning: it will not be easy. If you are willing to be truly free it will take integrity and fortitude the likes of which you have never conjured up in yourself until now. You must understand virtue in a culture that does not teach it. You will have to change the way you think and practice discipline if you're ever going to live a life of real freedom, the kind of freedom that our forefather's designed for us to live. You will have to take several major steps in a different direction if you are going to be set free of the bondage of the current financial culture. It will be painful, burdensome and difficult at first, but God never designed anything good in life that didn't come without some kind of suffering. Remember, it was the lie of a good feeling that got you into financial trouble to begin with. Once you apply a new strategy, you will find all the pain well worth it. There is an old saying, "If you find yourself in a hole, stop digging." With a little knowledge, determination and prayer, you too will become debt free.

I can look in your checkbook (or your credit card statement) and quickly tell you what kind a person you are. You would think me psychic, but the truth is people put their money exactly where their heart is. This is our belief system, and we will deposit our cash right into it. Whether it is vice or for the common good, it is what we believe in that we invest our money. And who we are is also determined by this belief system. *"As a man believes in his heart, so is he."* Christ Jesus spoke those words of wisdom 2000 years ago, and they shall always be true. This common fact accounts for the street person as well as the Wall Street Banker. This belief system can be holy or extremely evil, but it is a belief system all the same and it will determine how you live your life and where you will make your investments, what you will have, or not have and what you will do with all of it.

A fine example of how this works is clearly explained in a book called *The Top 10 Distinctions between Millionaires and the Middle Class* by Keith Cameron Smith. In this book, Smith defines the five classes of people in the United States and how their thinking affects their financial way of life. He breaks them down in the order of the very poor, the poor, the middle class, the rich and the very rich. I borrow some of his basic explanation with some adjusting of the numbers but go on to explain how each group of people "think" differently about money.

Very Poor people **think** day-to-day. Their primary goal is survival and they take in approximately $0 to $10,000 a year. They are the homeless, the unfortunate, the mentally ill, drug addicts, etc., and they will always be with us, and we are charged with their care.

The *Poor* **think** week-to-week or paycheck-to-paycheck. Their primary goal is also survival, and they too have a victim mentality. They make between $10,000 and $30,000 a year. They are immigrants, sometimes college students, single parents with children, and those with minimum wage jobs of which many depend on government entitlement programs and food stamps to survive, and most think they have no other choices in life. Many may live this way generationally.

The *Middle Class* **think** month-to-month and are enslaved to the monthly payment. Their primary goal is comfort. They make between $45,000 and $200,000 a year and make up most of the collective tax base. They are teachers, construction workers, firefighters, doctors, attorneys, professionals and the military among others. Most are deep in debt and depend on credit cards or revolving debt for survival. Because of easy credit systems, most middle class people live beyond their means through debt.

The *Rich* **think** year-to-year and make from $100,000 to $500,000 annually. Their primary goal is freedom. They are generally debt free and have learned the principles of fiscal responsibility, financial literacy and wealth. They too are teachers, police officers, doctors, etc. They have learned saving instead of spending and avoid debt at all costs. If they can't pay cash, they generally don't buy. They generally live below their means.

The *Very Rich* **think** decade-to-decade and generally have long term goals for their future and the future of generations to come and they understand the power in long-term thinking. Their primary goal in life is freedom, power, and influence. They are usually self-made and legally avoid many federal taxes through loopholes designed by their very influence upon policy makers. These people generally make over $500,000 a year.

So which class would you find yourself in? Why are you in it? Which class would you rather be in? If you noticed there is one key word that is used in every class of people above: "**THEY THINK.**" Each class of person **THINKS** a certain way and that determines where they end up in life . . . how they believe. That belief is based in knowledge and faith or lack thereof. Had I never studied personal finances, I would have never figured out how to become debt free and avoid the subsequent traps of the banksters. Once I began to accept a healthier way of thinking, then I began to **THINK** differently about my personal situation and began to set radical goals to change it. This is where real freedom lies, the freedom to make that choice.

I began to think in terms of "personal responsibility." I became free once I took responsibility for my money and personal control to do it my way. It takes work. If you are waiting to win that lottery or for some kind of government handout, well, that too is a belief system and sometimes our belief systems can be very unhealthy and dependent on worldly circumstances and systems. The bottom line is . . . *"Life is hard."* John Wayne even said, *"Life is hard, it's even harder if you're stupid."* I have to agree with big John because I lived stupidly for years until someone encouraged me to look at life differently, despite myself and all my excuses to avoid the pain of change. Basically, we go through life avoiding as much pain as possible by seeking comfort through means of debt, but sooner or later, we have to pay, and that is where the true misery begins. If you were wealthy, things could be different, right? The truth is, if you have a full time job or profession, you make wealth, you are wealthy, you just give it all away.

Yes, you make wealth! You make it every day and that wealth pays for very nice homes, luxury automobiles, prominent educations, wonderful vacations and summers in the Hamptons . . . but not for you. Yes, your wealth pays for all these things for those who have figured out how to get their hands on your hard earned cash. Like I said before, *"The world is designed to take your money,"* and it is doing so every day. Every day you make money. The problem is most people don't have a clue how to hold onto it. The key to making money is clearly understanding that it isn't all about what you make as much as **what you learn to keep**. Let me spell it out this way. Let's just say for argument that you earn a salary of $50,000 a year. Who gets it? That's right! Who gets it? Think about it and let that question soak in. If someone walked up to you and handed you 50,000 bucks, you would probably consider that a nice chunk of change. Well, that is what happens to you every year for a year at a time if you make $50,000 annually. So, where does it go? Who takes your money? Most likely, auto financiers, credit card companies, student loan institutions, mortgage companies, the US government, and any other financial predator. The world of money is a jungle, and if you do not figure out who the predators are they are going to devour you every chance they get. Knowing who is out for your money is extremely important in order to identify those predators.

I have learned to know where every cent of my money goes. Once you sit down and track your money, you will be amazed of how much you throw away on silly, non-essential items that the predators convinced you that you just had to have. The first step in getting out of the middle-class rat race is to understand where your hard earned dollars are going and do everything you can to stop the leaks and identify who is after your money.

I love Starbucks coffee and so does my wife. Occasionally, I will forgo a cup of joe at the house in order to treat myself to a hot cup of Starbucks Sumatra at a dollar and fifty six cents a cup. If I did this everyday of the year, I would spend over $560 annually, simply on coffee. I have to learn to say no to myself and have one cup of Starbucks coffee every two weeks and by doing so, it seems to taste so much better. The point here isn't Starbucks coffee but self-discipline.

You have to hold yourself accountable for your fiscal choices. Saying NO to your self is going to be instrumental in accumulating wealth. The first step to acquiring a life in the wealth column is to stop thinking monthly payments and start thinking year-to-year with your money, this is essential. If you don't, you will stay forever in debt to the predator creditors who will convince you that you need instant gratification and comforts every day of the year. You will continually belong to the monthly payment.

Once I understood the implications of looking at my finances on an annual basis, my entire life changed. By only getting Starbucks coffee once every two weeks instead of every day, I saved over 400 dollars, (remember the rabbits) which I now deposit into an IRA or mutual fund which over twenty years will net me a considerable amount of interest on my own money, making me wealthy instead of someone else. That is how we keep our hard earned dollar and turn it into wealth for ourselves instead of the bank. But let me be clear. Our goal is not to obtain worldly wealth and riches but rather to live a life of freedom from the beastly system which is deceiving the world.

Once again, know that the middle class lives for comfort. Comfort is expensive, and when one's life income isn't going up at the rate that corporate pay and bonuses are then that comfort must be obtained only through revolving debt. Some of you may be thinking, "I work so I should have stuff! After all, it's the American dream to have stuff . . . the pursuit of happiness and it's my right to spend if I want too." That is true, but if it is your understanding of life then you are, most likely, going to have a painful one. Remember, debt is a poor man's way of obtaining things he cannot afford.

Money and spending have a huge emotional and spiritual connection. The true IQ of a person may be his/her emotional IQ. Many very intelligent people are deep in debt because they lack emotional discipline. Many of these folks may have aced their college entry exams but were completely ignorant about how their emotions play on their fiscal lives. Practicing fiscal discipline is an emotional response to getting a handle on one's financial situation. It is a financially mature individual who understands finances in today's insane economy. Those in pursuit of happiness and comfort have made the fat banksters filthy rich. The first step of the wise is to understand that simply following the fiscal social trends will lead to debt, poverty and bondage to the financial institutions. They have figured out that our culture is telling us lies which are encapsulating the average American into a life of serfdom. As long as we keep spending, the guys on top continue to gain more and more power, control and influence over us as we spiral into the pits of hopeless debt.

In Matthew, chapter seven, Jesus teaches about the way to heaven: *"Enter by the narrow gate; for wide is the gate and broad is the way that leads to destruction, and there are many who go in by it. Because narrow is the gate and difficult is the way that leads to life and there are few who find it."*

We can say this same message applies to everything in our lives. As long as we avoid the road less travelled and live our lives for hedonistic pleasures which lack God's discipline, then wide is the gate we chose and destruction our just reward.

CHAPTER 6

THE OPPRESSORS

WE HEAR IT EVERY day, how to improve our FICO score. After all, FICO is what credit is all about, and we must maintain a high FICO score or else. And all of this is true if you believe that your life is all about debt then you need to worry about your FICO score. However, if you have been paying attention up to this point, you are beginning to understand, hopefully, that debt is the very thing we do not want in our lives, therefore, a FICO score should be mostly irrelevant. This concept is extremely difficult if not impossible for Americans to accept.

The FICO score is based 100% on your interaction with debt. It's about how much debt you have, the kind you have and whether you have new or old debt. It has absolutely nothing to do with your income or how much money you have in the bank or the kind of job you have or what a nice, responsible, law abiding citizen you are. It does not measure any success you have with money. It is a DEBT score, plain and simple. The only way to have a FICO score is to stay in debt. If you live debt free, then you do not have to worry about a FICO score. But what if one wants to buy a house, a car, start a business, etc.? You can do all that without the mark of the beast. You just have to spend time in the books learning ways not taught by the banksters. If you have a steady income and pay your bills, there are organizations that will do business with you. And, if it pleases you, once you successfully complete debt-free status through hard work and discipline, you can keep one credit card, just one, to use for something like gas expenses that you can easily pay off each month just to keep that FICO score up and thumb your nose at the credit reporting system.

What exactly is FICO? Glad you asked, time for FICO 101 as seen by a regular guy. Fair Isaac Corporation is a company that collects data on every single American consumer. If you have ever purchased anything on credit, you have a FICO score. The Fair Isaac Corporation Scoring Model is specific to that company and how they calculate your credit score. This score is then sold or incorporated into FICO's three offspring credit bureaus: Experian, Equifax and TansUnion. Your score or information may be calculated differently by each as each use different gathering vehicles, but generally different weights which add up to 100% are given to different categories of credit history, credit application, how much credit you use compared to that which is available, debt to pay ratio and a host of other values most which are secret and unexplained to the general public. This information is then sold for profit for various reasons to different industries. Ever wonder how all of those marketing companies get your address or home phone number? Now you know.

The actual FICO score usually ranges from about 350 to 850 with the upper numbers being representative of a very good credit rating. This doesn't just represent someone's pattern of good bill paying but rather how well they interact with debt. You may pay all your bills right on time but if you don't use credit cards or other sources of revolving debt on a regular basis, then you may have a much lower credit score than you would expect. The lower the credit score the higher interest you will be charged when borrowing money, and borrowing money is what we Americans are all about in order that we may have stuff. Remember, the FICO score is not about how much money you make or how good a person you are. It is a score that tells the financiers how well you play the debt game.

The Fair Isaac Corporation, FICO, was founded in 1956 by Engineer Bill Fair and Mathematician Earl Isaac in California. The company went public in 1987 and moved to Minneapolis Minnesota. They now have offices in Asia Pacific, Australia, Brazil, Canada, China, India, Korea, Malaysia, and the United Kingdom. The corporation provides analytics and decision making software including credit scoring intended to help financial services in gathering info on would be consumers and customers.

FICO sells other products such as decision management applications, analytics, corporate decision tools, scoring solutions and other professional services but is most known for its measure of credit risk on the general public throughout the United States and now into the rest of the world. If you have purchased anything on credit in the last 30 years, you have a credit score which gives you a financial and purchasing value as a human being.

As mentioned, the FICO score is available through three major credit scoring agencies in the US and Canada, Equifax, TansUnion and Experian. FICO provides its services and products to very large businesses and corporations in various fields: banking, insurance, retail, healthcare and life sciences.

A credit score is a numerical expression based on statistical analysis of a person's credit files which represent the "creditworthiness" of that person. The score is primarily based on credit reporting information gathered from the three major bureaus. Lenders such as banks and credit card companies use credit scores to evaluate risk posed by lending money to consumers and mitigate losses due to bad debt. Lenders use credit scores to determine who qualifies for a loan at what interest rate and at what credit limits. Lenders also use credit scores to determine which customers are likely to bring in the most revenue, giving them the ability to market those clients. Many companies are now using the credit score during background searches on potential employees as many believe that bad credit to be a sign of a probable problem employee.

Wikipedia identifies FICO as "a publicly-trade corporation" (under the ticker symbol FICO) that created the best-known and most widely used credit score in the US. In actuality, disregarding some other in-house vehicles used by a few credit card and mortgage companies, FICO is the only company of its kind and pretty much corners the market on personal information.

FICO's biggest partner Equifax works in complete parallel with FICO. In 1970, a company by the name of "Retail Credit Company" had been collecting information on people since 1899 and recommending to companies who and who not to do business with, for a price of course. In that year, 1970, Columbia Professor Alan Weston attacked the company in a New York Times article claiming that retail company files may include facts, statistics, inaccuracies and rumors about virtually every phase of a person's life including one's childhood, school history, career moves, marital troubles, sex life and political activities.

The article prompted congressional hearings that gave birth to the Fair Credit Reporting Act giving Americans the right to view and dispute their credit reports. The de-funked company, Retail Credit reformed under a new and industrious name known as Equifax in 1975. They have grown into the world's largest credit reporting organization. Their function is to collect as much information on us in any way they can most likely to sell that information with annual revenues of 1.3 billion dollars.

If you use the internet, you are constantly marketed with someone telling you how important it is to know your credit score and will direct you to a free credit score page. By law, each credit reporting organization has to provide you with information on your credit history for no charge, once a year. But, they do not have to disclose your credit score and they will not. They will only show you your credit history. The score itself will cost you usually just under $10 to be paid to the trickster who advertised that you could get your "free credit score." Remember from the chapter on advertising that nothing about most modern advertising is honest.

And you thought you were a free and independent American. Big brother is alive and well and making sure you follow his rules or suffer the consequences. So, let's get this right. If one wants to make a debt purchase in this country, he must first be scrutinized worthy of such trade before he can make the purchase based on his interactions with the debt beast. Correct! Not exactly what our founding fathers had in mind. Our founding fathers didn't create a system of perpetual debt either and warned us frankly of a world where commerce and corporate banking was all that mattered. We now must live with this beast and its oppressive instruments such as FICO and the credit scores.

Fortunately there is hope, and that is learning to live debt free. If that is your goal, then you do not have to live under the rule of the FICO score. Paying with cash sure beats a banker telling me what I can and cannot do with my life. The beast is hungry and you are the prey unless you learn the skills necessary to survive in the financial world, the first being a basic understanding of your responsibilities with your earnings.

When it comes down to it, an honest man pays his bills as best he can. A wise man pays with cash and cares less about some silly oppressive system designed to judge us by our mistakes or misfortunes in life. People are not a simple tool used only for commerce to be found worthy or not by some computer generated software. People make mistakes and a divorce or health crisis can financially devastate anyone. It is a nightmarish thought to know that some worldly institution holds one's human value based on his purchasing number. A most despicable thought to say the least. How did we ever get this way as a nation? On a slippery slope my friend, on a slippery slope.

Today's system of perpetual debt has created huge burdens on everyone. It is "as a hungry lion," lurking about in its attempt to devour those who do not understand its predator like intentions. If you do not understand the predator, it will be you he sneaks up on at the watering hole.

It is time to take a closer look into the lies we believed that got us where we are today. Let's look at the fibs that certain institutions created to separate us from our hard earned cash and enslaved us into the grips of the debt beast. Who are they that conspired to steal our livelihoods by creating cradle-to-grave consumers and money spenders who were fooled into believing that they lived in a nation where they were free? It's time to take a look at our captors, the offspring of the beast, the financial predators.

CHAPTER 7

THE OLE' COLLEGE SCAM

"We expect that all our children should graduate high school and college so they can all get good paying jobs." – President Barack Obama.

THIS IS A WONDERFUL concept and well intended, but it leaves one very important question to ponder for a regular guy. Who is going to do all the bad paying jobs? In a utopian world, such a statement would have merit as there would be no bad paying jobs, but in the real world there are a lot of bad paying jobs and jobs that require manual labor, difficult working conditions with no education and no skill requirements. Now, perhaps you are getting some idea how 12 million Mexicans walked into our country with very little government intervention. Because there is a market for them, a need in which low wages can be paid to do perceived meaningless jobs that our teenagers used to do.

Our teens, in general, are busy readying themselves for a future in college so they can be part of that group that will get better paying jobs. The problem is many of those better paying jobs no longer exist. Remember chapter one, corporate profits for the top percent of employees along with cheaper labor and a global economy are having serious consequences on the US job market. A high percentage of college kids are now leaving universities with an average debt of approximately $24,000 to $60,000 in student loans and moving back in with Mom and Dad because they can't get a job like the university systems assured would be waiting with open arms.

"Those who get a four-year degree generally make one million more dollars in their lifetime than those who do not." Hilary Clinton

This is part of the education lie. Yes, it is a lie. Not necessarily from Hilary Clinton, rather from the education system. This may be true for Wall Street investors, but it has not been true for the average working Joe. A lot of lies have been centered around education over the last twenty years such as, "Education will end poverty" or "It will guarantee a better life" or "The more money we throw into it, the better we'll be as a nation." I am not saying that a college education can't be a very useful tool in life, but I am saying that the reasons we give for an education today are mostly inflated theories designed to sell America on a deal that is leaving college grads in deep debt before they even have a job. And who's selling this stuff? You guessed it, the banksters. There is this crazy idea that no one questions, at least not until they are out of college, deep in debt and jobless, that has convinced Americans that they must have a college degree to be successful in life, no matter the price. But, thanks to outrageous costs associated with obtaining a college degree, the average family cannot afford to send their son's and daughter's to school. But not to worry, Uncle Sam and the banks are here to help.

Enter Fannie-Mae and the US government. Guaranteed secure loans for the want-to-be college graduate. Fannie-Mae was created during the Roosevelt administration to assist home owners in obtaining that first home but was expanded in the 1960's to also assist individuals in obtaining a college education. Once it was discovered that the college degree was marketable, Fannie-Mae left the ranks of the governmental programs and struck out on her own to create a very profitable business. Once the government "guaranteed" all student loans, the college education became a commodity, and universities across the nation suddenly saw the dollar signs. Tuition began to sky-rocket and administrative college ranks began to swell as more and more American college students began taking those loans with a guarantee by the college board of America that a brighter future was to be had, and the loans could always be deferred until that high paying job could be secured.

But something happened. Many of those entrusted students began defaulting on those loans so Fannie-Mae started her own financial collection agency. And with the US government guaranteeing payments on those loans, Fannie-Mae would automatically receive at least 25 percent from those loans in receivership. Like the banks on Wall Street, the federal government, which is another word for your tax dollar, has guaranteed financing for an industry on the way up and on the way down. The banksters profit again on the livelihoods of the working class via free money from the government money pool.

Over 6 million college students in America were awarded 56 billion dollars in financial aid in 2009 via Fannie Mae and the private sector. And it is no wonder in a culture that lives in perpetual debt to continue the Wall Street cash cow. Room, board, lectures, lab fees, transportation, food, etc., can cost the average college student approximately 60,000 to 100,000 real dollars for a four year degree. Most families do not have that kind of money but don't worry. Companies such as Fannie-Mae and a slew of other private banks are there to help and with Uncle Sam promising to back up those loans, college enrollments have increased dramatically over the last ten years.

And colleges love it, too. The guarantee of endless government funds has continued to allow college tuition to rise at an incredible 5.9 percent or more a year, although the rate of inflation is only averaging 3.3 percent annually. The truth is if no one guaranteed loans to college students, no self-respecting bank would loan them a dime. Would you? No one in their right mind would loan money to an age group whose frontal lobe hasn't fully developed. And because inflation isn't a good way to gauge for rising costs in education, universities have created "The Higher Education Index," a fancy term that means more money for banks and more debt for you and millions of college students who slowly come to terms that they have been lied to by an exploiting system.

Unfortunately, in our corporate climate of globalization, the college education has become big business with profits for those in the right places both in and out of the university systems. Convincing America that education is the end-all of our lively concerns is outrageous but talk to the average middle-class American parent and you will find them convinced that the college degree is a must. So, with that belief system secure under their belts, off they will go to the nearest college financial aid office where they will be sold a massive bill of goods designed to further rip-off their consumer-minded pocket books. No one is turned away when Uncle Sam is promising to pay . . . no one.

College, just like everything else in our over-consuming culture has become a product for profit for the big banks. In 1977 the average annual cost of college tuition was approximately $655. In 2007, it was $6,185, an increase of about 940 percent. In 1810, a year at Yale would cost the student $33 a year. By 1874, that tuition had increased to a whopping, $160. Today, one year at Yale will cost the student (or his parents) $36,500 all so one can be a "Yale Man," and that doesn't include the cost of housing, transportation and meals. The average four-year state college today will cost about $6,300 a year just for tuition and fees. Throw in the necessary room and board and tack on another $10,000. Then there's books and accessories (hidden costs) which could run upwards of an additional $3,000, and now we're talking truthfully about the real cost of college. The College Board justifies the cost of approximately $24,000 a year at a state sponsored school as "investing in oneself." Starting your professional life out with $60,000 to $100,000 in debt with no job is hardly investing in yourself.

The College Board says that the average college graduate will earn $22,600 a year more than high school grads. This, of course completely ignores the reality of dollars racked up in debt by the average college student who will not see that $50,000 a year job materialize and will spend four to five years learning and not earning as he or she racks up thousands of dollars in debt to finance a lifestyle which must be paid back to very wealthy interest craving banks.

So, how did we get in this outrageous situation where education is concerned? Well, as per the opinion of a regular guy, the current education situation really took hold in America by the 1970's when a social trend developed within emerging corporate America which assumed that in order for employees to promote within the corporate environment, it would be best that they have a "well rounded" education which could only be found at four year universities and colleges.

This idealism based in our primary education systems would structure brighter and better prepared corporate executives and staff in order for companies to compete in a growing world market. Regardless of the fact that such a notion was totally out of sorts with the spirit of our forefathers. But since we have become a status-driven culture, the ideology caught on because, in theory, it sounded so proper for the times. This, in turn, created a type of "educational elite" mentality across the country giving way to the suppression of entrepreneurialist thinking. It was always said that the father of invention is desperation but when invention and creativity are consumed or imprisoned by cultural roadblocks in the workplace then an entire nation, sooner or later, will reap in a lean harvest.

What America began to see by the 1990's was a workforce of over-educated and under skilled baby boomers and generation X'rs who outsourced an entire industrialized giant to third world countries in order to fill the coffers of the corporate elite. Through this process, many self-made and inventive individuals were forced out to make it on their own as college-degreed corporate snobs tossed them away as having little or no corporate value. The idea that one is not corporately useful if one has no college education is a social attitude born in the minds of stupidity and arrogance. The history of America will prove that it was not the Harvard business degree, but rather the ingenious minds of opportunistic determination, talent and intelligence coupled with the ability to meet human needs that made us the greatest nation the world had ever seen. It is extremely important to understand that freedom of the creative mind, guided by the discipline of social order is paramount to the growth of a nation. Any attempt to stifle that determination with intellectual prejudice as placing limits on this freedom in the workplace is most suppressive and is beginning to cost us dearly.

It is a downright lie to tell anyone they have less value in the workplace without a college degree. Many very successful and productive people paid no attention to the need for a college education. John D. Rockefeller, owner of Standard Oil, was America's first billionaire and one of the world's wealthiest men. He dropped out of high school. Bill Gates and Paul Allen, co-founders of Microsoft, both dropped out of college and are two of the wealthiest people in America today. The likes of these people either never graduated college or never even got there; George Washington, Abe Lincoln, Walt Disney, Peter Jennings, Chuck Yeager, Anthony Robbins, Mary Kay Ash, Coco Chanel, Thomas Edison, Orville & Wilber Wright, Rush Limbaugh, Lance Armstrong, Eleanor Roosevelt, Frank Lloyd Wright, Ansell Adams, Louis Armstrong, Tom Anderson, John Jacob Astor, Jane Austin, Irving Berlin, Furruccio Lamborghini, Michael Dell, Picasso, Earnest Hemmingway, Walter Cronkite, Andrew Jackson, Henry Ford, Ralph Lauren, Rachael Ray, Charles Dickens, George Foreman, Ben Franklin, Robert Frost, David Geffen, George Gershwin, J. Paul Getty, John Glenn, Barry Goldwater, Tiger Woods, Walt Whitman, Mark Twain, Harry Truman, William Shakespeare, Vidal Sassoon, Wolfgang Puck, George Orwell, Horace Greeley, William Randolph Hearst, Haroldson S. Hunt, Steve Jobs, Charles

Lindbergh, Herman Melville, Claude Monet, Florence Nightingale, George Bernard Shaw, Zachery Taylor, Dave Thomas, Cornelius Vanderbilt, and on, and on, and on.

Steve Jobs, creator of Apple and owner of Pixar Films, among other things, was an adopted child and college drop-out whose hard work, intelligence, and ability to see a need in the world made him one of the wealthiest men in modern America. Thousands and thousands of very successful business people today never graduated with a four year degree because they understood the world around themselves and instead of making excuses, endured the never ending tide of obstacles to overcome the pitfalls of life. These people understood hard work and determination and were able to create their own opportunities in life or go hungry. They were risk takers determined to make it or live with the consequences, foregoing any conjectured guarantees offered by the modern education system. That is what our forefathers had in mind when they created a nation where the average person would always have that opportunity. The lack of financial guarantees created a thirst for survival and success.

Life will never guarantee anything and will most likely push your will to the best of your ability, and then it will mold you into something strong if you allow it. Over the years, many have done just that, and the skills that life has given them are extremely valuable and certainly nothing that they would have learned in college. We are now experiencing the rude awakening of a generation who expected that life, through government support, would hand them a future based upon inflated theories designed by social educators and the bankers who profited from their misguided adventures.

Please let me be clear one more time. I am not telling people to ignore an education. Education is paramount in the proper perspective and will eventually be a valuable asset in life. I am advising to weigh the facts before jumping into something that has been sold to the general public as an extremely expensive necessity when it simply is not, and advertising an impression that those with no college education will not succeed is a lie.

College is actually a risky investment that may never pay off. Perhaps fifty percent of people in the workforce end up working in positions or fields that do not even pertain to their specific degree. Our current advanced education system tells you to invest in yourself by getting that college degree and life will be grand. The question each of you has to ask is, is it really worth it in today's financial climate?

It may be best that most graduating high school seniors actually stay out of college for two to three years and obtain some serious life skills before jumping into the college debt scam. Many see college as a must, but a recent survey revealed that 40 percent of graduated college students would not repeat the adventure given their current situation while strapped with outrageous student loan dept. And, more and more college students are graduating while lacking critical thinking abilities or complex reasoning skills after years of costly study.

"The Bachelor's degree is America's most over-rated product," says career counselor Dr. Marty Nemco in a recent report by ABC's 20/20. He went on to say, "It's been my observation to see that most successful college grads would have been successful anyway, with or without a college degree. Hard work, persistence and intelligence are the key. Statistically, if you are in the bottom 40 percent of your high school class then the chances of you making it through to graduating a university system is very low. Most are left in debt and very disappointed and unfortunately, this is the type of student who is being sold on the college idea."

Susie Orman, author of several books on personal finances and host of her own syndicated television show says, "College is great for those with the smarts to become doctors, lawyers and scientists but most should reconsider their futures and the value of the general bachelor's degree. It is much more important in today's work environment to acquire specific marketable skills at a local community college for a fraction of the cost. Technical schools or apprentice programs within certain companies are becoming more and more valuable." Jobs such as police officers, teachers, nurses, mechanics and other vocational professions are always going to be consistent and needed. Unfortunately, vocational schools or trade schools are looked down upon because we are a status driven society where many believe that prestigious careers are the key to a life well lead and it often isn't the case.

We see some today that are so in debt to college loans that they see no light at the end of the tunnel. Some, especially those with advanced degrees, are in debt to a tune of $150,000, and it isn't uncommon to see medical students with student loans that exceed $200,000. And to add insult to injury, top dogs within the university systems all across America are jumping on the CEO compensation wagon as the university systems reflect more of the corporate mentality by giving financial compensation homage to the top guys.

More and more college and university presidents are being paid well over the million dollar mark, especially in the last five years and of course, university and College Board members and associates defend these salaries and perks as "crucial to their success as a center of higher learning." After all, some academic's argue, "High compensation for those at the top reflects the growing demand for skilled people from a shrinking population of qualified leaders." Sounds more like someone barking for a job on Wall Street. The only ones believing the CEO pay mentality are the ones who benefit from it or those foolish enough to buy snake oil. Unfortunately, such overzealous compensation has spawned a new upper-class within academia that grows steadily disconnected from the masses and undermines public confidence in our higher education system.

Our current system of higher education has turned into a huge scam brought to you by the same makers of Rue de Wall and associate partner, Uncle Sam, a perfect example of government intervention that sends prices through the roof. One of the best political campaigns made by politicians is to aid student education. A well intended idea unfortunately went awry when the government attempted to make education affordable to all by creating a loan market that every student and family could use to further their education. But greed got involved and tuition continues to rise. College tuition, on average, rose approximately seven percent in 2009, even in the midst of the worst recession in 80 years. In 2012, college tuition will rise another 5.2 percent, a fifty four percent increase over the past ten years with absolutely no common explanation as to why. The burden to meet that cost is upon you.

A large amount of employers will not hire recent college graduates. Only 20 percent of graduating college seniors will have a job within six months of graduating. The other 80 percent have no money, no job and, on average, a monthly tuition bill of approximately $400 for at least the next ten years. While the starting salary for the college grad is between $32,000 and $49,000 annually, 10 percent of that will go to pay those student loans for a very long time. Thousands of waiters in the restaurant business have college degrees but can't find that long anticipated career in the business sector.

Once again, you have to ask yourself, is it worth the investment of four to five years of your life and sinking yourself, on average, to $24,000 in debt to be paid back with interest in the next ten to twenty years? This current system is not working. Instead of opportunity, the typical college student is being led to the slaughter and strapped with mind-numbing debt. Basically, we're being educated in Debt 101 as the bankers, who loan money out of thin air, become wealthier off the backs of the working class.

But life in college isn't all bad; the average freshman will spend approximately $700 on books and $900 on beer. Party school reputations are rampant across America, and there is always Spring Break where literally millions of American college kids head south to resorts that cater especially to their party needs, mostly all paid for by credit cards from jobless party goers as this ridiculous educational right-of-passage is annually celebrated nationwide. More sexually transmitted diseases are contracted during the month of March in America among the collegiate age group than any other time of the year, by far. But that's ok, their just kids having fun.

Because of the dumbing down of the American education system in the last 30 years, not many kids are able to become doctors and engineers but mention a party and that is one thing we Americans can respect and do better than anyone else in the world, and we'll do it all on debt. Recently I saw a bumper sticker that read, "My son is serving in the US Marines, so yours can party in college." A sad reminder of what our education system delivers. In short, the average college education does not give the student any practical knowledge for life in general, like how to get an education without becoming a slave to the banks. Employers want people with some kind of life and work experience and a strong work ethic, not some kid who is a master at video games toting a generic bachelor's degree but knows nothing of life in the workplace, unskilled, covered with tattoos, and deep in debt.

Unfortunately, the American system of higher education has gone the way of corporate profit. One must educate him or herself about the current culture of the predator bankers before ignorantly jumping into the college game. There are many ways to avoid becoming entangled in the education lie via the debt spider web. The best thing going out there is the local community college. The average cost for tuition and fees at the local public community college or trade school is about $2,300 a year.

Most students at two-year schools will not be living on campus so room and board are not as much a factor, here again, saving the student thousands of dollars annually. Trade schools hold endless opportunities, and the skills learned in those schools are extremely necessary to our society. For example, to become a professional firefighter in the state of Texas requires two certifications. One is the basic firefighter's certification through the Texas Commission on Fire Protection, and the other is the Emergency Medical Technician certification by the Department of Health. The student will invest two college semesters to obtain these certifications at a cost of about $3,000. Then they are eligible to test for a position with a municipality within the state of Texas. Some larger cities start rookie firefighter salaries at around $40,000 to $50,000 annually. A degree will not help land a job in this profession. The higher education only helps when advancing into administrative positions later in one's career. Many career firefighters return to college later to obtain the necessary education for job advancement and usually do so without incurring any debt.

Another option, as briefly mentioned earlier, is to wait until later before going to college. This concept will help one obtain excellent experience in the workplace in which they will appreciate the importance of obtaining the right kind of degree instead of just going off to college because that is what all their friends are doing. This will also help one work and save for college instead of going into debt with outrageous student loans. There are also work programs that students can become involved in while in college that will help pay for tuition.

Then, there are thousands and thousands of available scholarships just waiting on the right person. These, however, do require some work on the part of the student to obtain. These will require good grades to be eligible and mostly go to the top percent of students, but they are out there and thousands of organizations exist that are just aching to give them away. Good grades are a must for the serious high school student who wants to go the route of the scholarship. This is especially advisable to those who plan on becoming engineers or physicians or the like.

"There are two educations; one should teach us how to make a living and the other how to live." John Adams

In 1940 a young man from Texas joined the army after two years of college at Texas A&M University. He wanted to fly and was accepted into the US Army Air Corps Cadet Training Program. He grew up on a farm near the town of Stephenville where times were hard especially during his early teens as the great depression set in. He had no idea how his harsh upbringing would prepare him for what was to come. After his initial training in San Antonio, which he found terribly difficult, he made the cut and continued on to advanced bomber training in Nebraska where he was assigned a plane and a crew and then off to Rhode Island for further training before shipping off to England as part of the American 8th Air Force.

Soon he found himself the pilot of a brand new B-17 bomber, a "flying fortress" as they were called, with nine men under his command. He would fly 52 missions over Germany and France during WWII in a large plane full of bombs, fuel, and the lives of nine of his best friends . . . he was 22 years old. The challenges of a hard life on the farm, a little college and the horrors of war gave him an education he would remember all his life. Could the average college boy today be entrusted with such responsibility? because in 1941, thousands had to be. Can American colleges prepare this kind of a person any longer?

Over all, the face of America is changing and we must change with it. The old days of going to college, getting a degree and landing a great paying job right out of school, are over. America needs engineers, doctors and scientists, and our current culture of education simply isn't preparing our youth for that kind of mission. An advanced education will serve those right who obtain it to further their current professional needs, but just getting a degree to get a degree isn't helping people any longer, and it is starting young people off in untold debt at a time in their lives when they should be making money and creating a foundation for life. Unfortunately, very wealthy predator lenders have found a way to steal the American dream away from would be producers before they can even produce.

Only practical knowledge before collegiate knowledge can help one avoid the traps of these predators.

One has to weigh the facts. Is a college degree worth the debt? Being strapped with a mountain of debt isn't the way to start off one's life. Millions of young Americans are being lied to and unfortunately don't figure it out until it's too late.

In closing, my advice to young people is to weigh your options and never be afraid to challenge the world with the gifts, talents and passion God gave you. Hard work, dedication and persistence will be your best allies in your career but know that if you're only looking into a life of monetary reward, you may find yourself sorely disappointed.

CHAPTER 8

THE CAR PAYMENT

BY THE BEGINNING OF the 20th century and the height of the industrial age, the horseless carriage was born. Stepping into the petroleum age was phenomenal in this country. Most people, however, couldn't afford an automobile until an inventive entrepreneur changed that. American icon, Henry Ford, revolutionized the country by building a car that most Americans could purchase. His idea of the modern assembly line changed transportation as well as industry forever. President Eisenhower furthered the future of transportation by creating the US interstate system allowing freedom and affordability for Americans to travel from one place to another. Ever since, Americans have been in love with the automobile.

But, love or not, as we read earlier, the cost for cars has risen approximately 54 percent since 1970. This is a discerning fact for a regular guy. The problem is the average home income has virtually remained the same based on affordability and inflation, so one would think owning that nice car would be difficult. Not at all, thanks to modern banking, which has made the availability for ownership of vehicles very possible. Today, almost anyone can obtain the car of his dreams thanks to auto credit programs. But, truth be known, automobiles are one of the worst investments on the planet, and in no other arena do Americans throw away more money than on cars. Because of easy credit, car loans are a huge burden on the American family.

Here is how this regular guy views the auto sales industry. The average automobile loses approximately 60 percent of its value over four years. Just driving a new car off the lot can mean an immediate twenty five percent drop in its worth. Not a good way to save money. However, most Americans are very under-informed where buying a vehicle is concerned. If one thing the reader must understand it is this . . . the words "deal" and "car" are absolutely not synonymous. There is rarely such a thing as a "good deal" for the buyer when a car purchase is made, though the phrase has been used by auto sales professionals for years. This is simply an advertising ploy, and we all know by now that there is no honesty in advertising. This is not to say that every car dealer is a crook. Many attempt to do business on the up and up, but the very nature of their business has left the industry with a less than honorable reputation. The fact is cars are just too expensive.

For years, the automobile industry has been intimidated and operated by heavy union influence resulting in very decent pay and benefits (mainly increasing health care obligations) for assembly line employees while paying out huge salaries and benefits to top end executives at the other end of the spectrum. Not to say that the people building the cars shouldn't share in the wealth of the business, but consistent outrageous demands by autoworker unions became a serious blow to the auto industry. Jobs and careers are extremely important but when the product they produce becomes a burden for the masses because of cost, then an industry becomes tarnished. Unfortunately, years of this process has devastated cities like Detroit as auto makers either went broke or moved their assembly plants to other countries.

Cars are a reflection of who we are or for many, or who we want people to think we are. There was a time when a car was a means of transportation but now days, the car is used as much as a status symbol as it is a way to get from point a to point b and many will foolishly spend money they do not have to obtain that status symbol. Some people are so engrossed with the status symbol that they pay as much monthly for the cars as for the house. Many people are living paycheck to paycheck in order to drive that status symbol. We've all seen neighborhoods where there is a small run down house with three to four very nice cars outside. Some believe that paying 40 to 50 thousand dollars for a vehicle is a must to maintain an overindulgent lifestyle that they cannot afford.

Recently, a local banker revealed to me that he has turned down many would-be customers who were bent on owning the car of their dreams regardless of the cost. Many, he reported, have such bad credit that they couldn't get a loan for a car if their life depended on it. Another loan officer once told me that he worked with a woman for two days to get her into her dream car. Her credit was so bad that he was having a difficult time finding a finance company that would take a risk on her. She, however, was so insistent that he finally located a company that specialized in high risk/high interest auto loans resulting in a 26 percent interest on the loan once all was implemented. The woman, who obviously had no clue about finances, was absolutely beside herself when told she qualified for the car. That was ten years ago and she's probably still making payments.

Regardless, an automobile is a must in today's culture. We have to have transportation to get to work, get the kids to school, buy groceries, and many people today commute from city to suburb and back daily. But, we don't have to live with a monthly automobile payment of 600 dollars or more for six years which we are seeing today. Many are doing so just to drive that ego car, all the while robbing from Peter to pay Paul. That, my friend, is all hat and no cattle.

The average new car today will cost from 25 to 30 thousand dollars. The average value of the trade-in vehicle is never enough to offset the cost due to depreciation. The car dealer will always want a lot more than his car is worth and will never offer you what you think yours is worth. That is the nature of the business. What to do? You have no choice. You have to finance the car. Hello, auto financing! If there is one thing I learned a long time ago it is that GMAC is not a car company. It is a finance company that uses cars to make money from unsuspecting victims such as me.

An elderly man once said that the worst accident he ever had was on a showroom floor. It's one thing to be ripped off on the lot, but the real rip off begins in the finance office. How about that undercoating for just an extra five hundred or that extended warranty? After all, everyone gets an extended warranty, right? The truth about an extended warranty tells me that the auto dealer doesn't put a lot of stock into his product. Let's take a look at the extended warranty. It's only an extra 35 dollars a month. You'll hardly notice it, and it will give you peace of mind knowing that your car will get repaired for free if it ever breaks down. The truth is, if I am buying a new car, it had better not break down for at least 100,000 miles or for the first four years. But the reality of the situation is cars do break down, even new ones. Besides, most new cars come with an automatic bumper-to-bumper warranty for 30,000 miles or three years and some up to 100,000 miles. Do not purchase that extended warranty!

The extended warranty, over the time of a six year note at forty five dollars a month will cost you over three thousand dollars. Also, anything wrapped into the monthly payment will be charged the interest on the note. Even if the transmission were to go completely out, it would cost you one third of the price. Extended warranties can be a rip off. One day while discussing this with a new car dealership owner, he told me he makes most of his profits on extended warranties. Many extended warranties do not cover everything. Just check the fine print regardless of what a dealership tells you. Remember, the attorney is always in the fine print to explain how that warranty covers everything except the part you need.

I work in a profession with many guys who drive four-wheel-drive pickups. It is an image in this part of the country, a reflection of "the cowboy, freedom and manlihood," though not one of them would admit it. A fact is four-wheel drive trucks are not cheap. The average four-wheel drive pickup runs around thirty five to forty five thousand dollars, "used". Some top of the line trucks can run over fifty thousand. That's more than I paid for my first house. Let's take a look at an example of today's car buying ritual below. For arguments sake, we'll go with a new four-wheel drive pickup for the low price of $37,000. Remember now, we are middle class people so we do not consider a sticker price, rather "affordable monthly payments". So, let's figure that we traded in our old beat-up used pickup which they naturally gave us $3,000 for. So, we really got a great deal by getting a $37,000 truck for only $34,000. Let's look at what it really costs to drive that truck for one year.

Sticker Price	$37,000.00
Trade in	$3,000.00
Actual Price	$34,000.00
Taxes	$3,052.50 @ 8.25%
Title and License	$482.67
Extended Warranty	$862.00
Total	**$38,397.17**

Now it's time for the financing at the market rate of 6.99% . . . a good deal!

Total (the real price)	**$46,080.00**

Now, since you're a middle class person, you don't make enough to make huge monthly payments but that's ok because, just like every friendly financier, the finance officer is going to get you into affordable monthly payments of $640 a month for 72 months. Now we're talking. Soon, you'll be cruising the highway in your new man-ride, and the girls are gonna think you're the cat's meow. But that's only the cost for the vehicle, not the actual annual operating cost. Something the average car buyer completely ignores. Remember, the wealthy think of their money on an annual basis, not on a monthly payment. The middle class think monthly payment and stay in perpetual debt. So let's look at the real annual cost of owning that $46,000 pickup.

Annual amount of automobile payment	$7,680.00
Insurance cost	$1,260.00
Fuel and Maintenance	$4,200.00
Total annual operating cost	**$13,140.00**

Total cost for this vehicle in six years (life of the note) $78,840.00

This is not exactly considered wealth building.

Now, let's check out the cost of buying a used Toyota Camry or Honda Accord under 50,000 miles.

Sticker Price	$15,500.00
Trade in	$3,000.00
Actual Price	$12,500.00
Taxes	$1,278.75 @ 8.25%
Title and License	$482.67
No Extended Warranty	$0
Total (the real price)	**$14,261.00**

After Financing at 6.99%	**$16,368.00**

Annual amount of payment (48 month note)	$4,092.00
Insurance cost	$540.00
Fuel and Maintenance	$2,650.00
Total annual operating cost	**$7,282.00**

Total cost for this vehicle in four years (life of the note) $29,128.00

The total cost to operate the used sedan for the life of the note is $29,128, while the total cost to operate the four wheel drive pickup for the life of its note was $78,840. That is a difference of **$49,712**. That is college tuition for your children or perhaps one quarter the cost of your home. Now I'm no rocket scientist, but it doesn't take a genius to figure those numbers. Now, if a fella were to take that amount and invest it in a compounded mutual fund account earning 6.5% a year for twenty years, he would net himself $179,665.00. But monthly payment folks don't do things like that, do we?

That is a lot of money, so perhaps you can see now why the middle class live month to month. A person who understands fiscal responsibility would never do business this way. That is why they are wealthy. The average millionaire doesn't drive big expensive vehicles with six year notes, rather they drive used sedans and take the difference and invest over time turning that $49,712 into hundreds of thousands or they simply pay cash because instead of blowing their hard earned dollars for years on expensive vehicles with insane interest payments, they practiced discipline, drove used affordable vehicles and saved their money.

Well then, what about leasing the car? You can drive a brand new car for two years on most lease programs and then trade it in on another brand new one for cheaper monthly payments. That way, you don't have to worry about wear and tear and depreciation. Right? Hold on before you head out to make your first "smart deal," as the industry calls it. It is a smart deal, for the dealer . . . not necessarily for you.

Consider this; you don't just get to lease a car. There is a contract involved and that means you must have some kind of deposit or down-payment. Your used car will usually do for the average three thousand dollar origination fee. Then you get to lease the car with monthly payments of only $350 for the next two years for a nice Lexus. But wait, did we mention that you can't go over 15,000 miles a year or you'll have to pay some kind of excess mileage charge. And in some states, there are other fees and transaction addendums on the backside of the deal. Then there is a depreciation costs, taxes etc. So, let's add up the deal. $350 a month, plus taxes for two years amounts to $8,400 plus the original $3,000 plus tax, title and license, and did I mention interest charge? In most states, the dealer doesn't have to disclose interest on a lease. The easy $350 "deal" is actually over $12,000 in just two years, and that doesn't count fuel, insurance, and maintenance, and you're also responsible for dings and dents. Then, when the deal is over, you don't have a car so you either sign another lease or buy another car with no trade in which will cost you the full sticker price. So much for rent-a-car smart deals!

"But hey, I got a rebate for buying a new car! I got $4,000 cash back." Ok, so you did, but the problem with most cash back programs are they are usually restricted to hard to move vehicles on the lot. The ones the manufacturer knows don't sell very well so they create a cash- back program to entice folks to believe they're getting a heck of a deal.

What about "zero" percent interest for the first year? A good deal! Remember Einstein, there is no such thing as a good deal in the auto business if you are on the paying end! Get that through your skull. The cash back is only for those who qualify. And who qualifies? Those with a credit score of 690 and above. And again, usually zero percent only applies to the vehicles on the lot that are hard to move and always know that "only certain qualified buyers are eligible." Car companies aren't in business to give you anything. Don't be fooled into believing they are making a deal for you because you are a special qualifying customer. You betcha! Because they truly care about you and your family! And, once you drive that brand new "deal" off the show room floor, it loses value and continues to do so every day.

The simple truth is a car is a product just like anything else used for a business to sell or lease for profit. And, just like any other form of business, those in the auto sales business are out to make a profit.

They know the ends and outs of their business and the tricks of their trade a lot better than the average guy or gal off the street including you and me. Many don't outright lie to you in the process. That would be dishonest. They just don't tell you all the things you need to know . . . which is still dishonest. The best thing to do is your homework before purchasing a vehicle. Remember any time a car dealer uses the word "deal" know that there exists a catch in there somewhere and in most cases, there are two or three. Cars are a must in today's hectic society and one can easily find him or herself upside down on an expensive car note and stuck with high payments that imprison the unaware car buyer for years and worse, rob them of wealth building money they could have otherwise used for a 401K.

But before we end this chapter on car buying, we must remember the "Tote the Note" guy. These car dealers are usually on the bottom of the car dealer food chain. The cars on their lots are usually the end of the line in the life of the average automobile. Many are predator dealers who charge outrageous interest rates and huge down payments to people with horrible credit. Unless you're recently released from a maximum security prison where you have been incarcerated for the last thirty years, you'll want to stay clear of these folks. They know that most of their customers can't or won't continue to make their car payments and since they hold the note, they legally own the car and quickly repossess them for resale to some other financially illiterate or desperate soul. Knowing what they are all about and how their business works should be part of your auto buying research.

In the last twenty years we have seen outrageous new car sales. Cars saturate our country but as times change and Americans are forced into a new reality of doing without, we could see more and more people keeping the family car for up to ten years on average rather than trading them in every two or three years.

The bottom line . . . cars are all about ego to most people. Just observe people once they are in their cars and cruising down the road. Some use the car for the purpose of transportation. Others use it as a status symbol, and those are the ones most likely deep in debt to look the part or to experience the comfort of that fine automobile. Don't be one of those. Know what you are doing and give up the self when it comes to a major need that could end up costing you thousands of dollars that should be going into your pocket and not to some finance company. There's nothing worse than being upside down in your payment (owing more than the vehicle is worth).

Average unsuspecting Americans ignorantly throw millions and millions of dollars into automobile interests annually thinking there is no other way to obtain a car. This simply isn't true. Understanding the auto industry from the top down is crucial to keeping them from taking your hard earned cash by making you believe there is no other way. A used Honda Accord or Toyota Camry can hold car seats just as well as a Tahoe or any other SUV. The smart car owner steers clear of the expensive big cars and takes the savings and puts it to work for him instead of the auto finance companies knowing that the faster a note is paid off, the less interest one will pay and interest, my friend, is the name of the financial game.

The key to saving on a car is to pay it off as soon as possible. That is difficult in today's car market as auto financers have stretched the payment system out for as many as 72 months. That was unheard of 20 years ago but today is an industry standard. The longer it takes to pay something off, the more you will pay in interest and interest to the bank is a theft of wealth from you and your family. DO NOT purchase a vehicle you can't afford to pay off early and for crying out loud, do not take a 72 month loan. Americans are throwing away money on cars by leveraging themselves to do it. Stay within your means when buying a car and know that making that emotional decision can cost you dearly.

CHAPTER 9

THE UNHOLY HOUSE PAYMENT

EVERYONE DESERVES A HOME; after all, every creature has a home. Beavers live in their dams, bees in their hives, bears in caves, and people in houses built mostly of brick, cement and wood. And good intentions lead us to believe that every American deserves "affordable" housing. The only problem with that concept is a problem that has become as American as apple pie and that is the fact that some people simply do not pay their bills and those folks usually have track records of such behavior. Ignoring that fact, many politicians believed that every American deserved to own a home and pressured the mortgage industry to make it happen, despite dire warnings from many experts of unfolding consequences. But many of the big banksters were more than happy to comply, resulting in the biggest housing bubble in American history. This debacle would eventually lead to the worst economic meltdown since the Great Depression. The result is a housing market that has flat-lined and thousands of Americans losing their homes because they couldn't afford the payments as they were completely ignorant of their payment plan or simply ignored the mathematical consequences of their desire for that dream house. So, how in the world did all this happen?

Well, from a regular guy's point of view, it's really quite simple and works like this. Many wealthy people or people who understand the way money grows are always looking for safe investment vehicles to grow their wealth. For years, government bonds were traditionally the best way to do so. Then, a man by the name of Allen Greenspan became Chairman of the Federal Reserve and began to lower interest rates year after year. This caused a mass exodus of investors looking for other means of monetary growth. The real estate market stepped up to the plate and became the place to dump investments during the 1990's into the 2000's as the price of homes skyrocketed across the nation. And just like any feeding frenzy, it wasn't long before the sharks arrived. Once Wall Street got involved, billions of dollars were being made and the game was afoot. Every major bank on Wall Street wanted a piece of the housing market and to insure their investments would continue to grow the mortgage industry, for the first time ever, became more and more relaxed ignoring traditional rules and regulations which were designed to protect the industry and the homebuyers. The industry began taking huge risks with people who could not afford a home yet, because of so much money being made at the top, it didn't matter. The feeding frenzy had begun and billions of dollars were being made regardless of the huge warning signs that the bubble was about to bust, and in September 2008, the entire thing went pop!

But, not to worry, the fat cats got bailed out by their partner in crime, the US Government. You, on the other hand, did not. Even though the company holding your note went broke you still have to pay. After all, someone has to pay, and its always going to be you, and if you do not understand the unspeakable dollars spent on your home mortgage over thirty years, you will continue to pay and pay and pay. Let's pull our head out of the sand and take a look at the truth about the home mortgage.

The house is the largest investment that most Americans will make in their lifetime. In 1910, only 2 percent of Americans had a home mortgage. By 1990, only 2 percent did not as the home mortgage industry came of age through the savings and loan market. Unfortunately, the savings and loan industry collapsed in the 1980's giving way to a new home mortgage industry which resulted in an explosion of mortgage loans by 2007. The home mortgage industry became a quagmire of profits for hungry profiteers making untold monies as they ignored all the warning signs of impending doom at the cost of homeowners.

If you remember earlier I explained how the mortgage works. The mortgage banker, once you have paid down 10 percent of the loan, whips the money out of thin air and places it into your account showing that they have loaned you said amount which is to be paid back over thirty years based on interest resulting in over two to three times the original loan amount. So, that $100,000 loan becomes a $203,000 loan over 30 years. Then add on home insurance and property taxes and the price is in reality closer to $300,000. Most people have come to accept this fact as the pain of getting into that home.

This plan unfortunately straps the average family with payments that net on average from $1,000 to $2,000 a month. That means $12,000 to $24,000 out of pocket annually for thirty years. That is going to take one third of one person's life salary to pay. Those who understand financial responsibility never do business that way, but the average American is ignorant of other options or simply does not care to understand the rules to fiscal responsibility.

Many Americans are under the misguided idea that they must own a brand new home with all the amenities, especially the younger, just married generation. Next to the student loan lie, this idea is the first step into the life-long debt trap. The truth is, there are thousands of small, older affordable homes on the market that can be purchased for a fraction of the cost of the new 2,300 square foot brick home. The savings is made over time. Purchasing a fixer-upper for under $100,000 can usually save a family thousands of dollars over several years. It is amazing what paint, a hammer and nails along with a manicured yard can do for a place. But this means that the home owner must get away from the television and do some work.

Let's say, for example, a young married couple purchases an older, 1500 square foot home for $90,000 on a fifteen year note. Then, since their home is affordable, they are able to make one extra payment each year. This act alone can knock off at least four years from the note allowing them to pay off their home within 11 years. So, instead of paying $203,000 over 30 years, they paid $107,000 or less, in 11 years and now own their home outright. Now, they have complete equity and can sell that house, probably for one and a half to two times what they bought it for and that, my friend, is a healthy down-payment on that dream home. Not to mention, they can use the same formula for the new home and pay it off soon, putting money back into their pockets or into a 401k plan instead of a mortgage company. Now, they are building wealth instead of being enslaved into their retirement years to a house payment. And that is how the wealthy think as do the debt free.

One of the biggest mistakes made by people is thinking that they must own a home right out of college. There is nothing wrong with renting. Most argue that renting is throwing money away. Hello!. So is buying a home on a thirty year note and paying two and a half times the loan value, all the while strapping a family into a paycheck-to-paycheck lifestyle. At least rent is cheaper than a house payment for ownership, and renters do not pay taxes or home insurance. Renters are not responsible for upkeep and home maintenance either. There is nothing wrong with renting for a time period. One should weigh the cost and rent cheaply if possible in order to save the difference for that down payment on the home to own.

Another big home buying mistake is the Adjustable Rate Mortgage or ARM. This idea was popular during the years when Jimmy Carter was President and the interest rates were hitting all time records of 15 to 18 percent. The idea of an adjustable interest rate was to attract people to buy homes with loans based on initial high interest that would surely drop once the rates adjusted every two to five years. But interest rates bottomed out by 2005 making the ARM no longer necessary until predator mortgage companies and banks used the same tactic to entice would-be home owners into qualifying for the home which many did not understand (this was the basis of the economic meltdown of 2008). The idea was to allow them a low qualifying monthly payment initially so they could get the loan. Then, the rate would hit its adjustment period and wham! The pigeon homebuyer saw his monthly payment double, taking him and his family to the cleaners. And, none of this mattered to the banker or mortgage company as they got their money up front. The homeowner had no equity built in the home and usually couldn't sell, so the home went into foreclosure or short sale. ARM's are not a smart way to buy a home. As a matter-of-fact, they are perhaps the worst idea ever pushed on the American public by greedy mortgage and real estate companies. Anyone who would recommend an ARM should be arrested or at least locked up and forced to listen to constant 70's era disco music as punishment for their sin.

Many people will refinance their home mortgage several times over the course of the loan in order to continue lowering their monthly payment. This is a huge and costly mistake. One should never, ever refinance a loan unless it is to their financial benefit. If you wish to refinance from a 30 year mortgage to a fifteen year fixed rate mortgage, that is a good move if you plan to stay in that home, especially if you haven't been paying on the note for more than four to five years because you are saving thousands of dollars in the long run. Or, if you wish to refinance to get out of an ARM or any other adjustable rate mortgage, go for it. But know that the mortgage company will act as if they're doing you a favor while all along knowing that they start with their interest costs right up front, and once again you will be paying mostly interest for the first seven years of the loan. That is one you will have to weigh depending on the savings you should or should not receive by refinancing. And know that when refinancing, someone has to pay fees and closing costs. Make sure that the cost is figured into the entire deal to see if it financially benefits you in the long run.

If there is one rule every single home owner should never break it is never, ever take out a home equity loan. This is insane. Your home is your most important asset. Taking out a home equity loan is simply creating two house payments. Why would anybody want to do that? Be very careful about mortgage companies tempting you to do so. Even if your home is paid for, it is a huge mistake to go back into debt on a home mortgage again via a home equity loan.

Another lie I have been told about home ownership was the crazy concept that if I paid off my home, I would lose my tax break on what I pay in interest. Hmm? The guy who thinks that way can't do simple math. For example, if my property taxes are $2,300 annually then I get a small tax credit on my interest paid each year, as long as I am paying interest. But remember, most interest is paid on the first 10 years of the note anyway so one doesn't get much of a tax break after 10 years of making payments. Then, if I am making $1,000 payments on my home loan every month that is $12,000 annually. So, which do I want to pay, $2,300 annually for full taxes or $12,000 annually to get that little bit of tax break? You do not have to be Albert Einstein to figure the math on that one. That is some of the most foolish advise I was ever given. Pay off the house as soon as possible because it alone is stealing more of your wealth than any other investment you have.

One more home item I should cover before closing this chapter is a warning about purchasing mobile homes or manufactured homes. The cost of a mobile home is half the price of a traditional residential structure and argued by some to fit the monetary lifestyles of those who cannot afford that traditional brick home. Think again. You can purchase a mobile home for $60,000, which is true. What the mortgage company and the mobile home or manufactured home salesman failed to tell you was the home will lose its value just like an automobile. Five years later, the new mobile home or manufactured home will be worth half of what you paid for it yet you will still be strapped with paying the entire mortgage for years to come.

Another issue with these structures is the fact that they are traditional fire traps and tornado magnets. They are made of less than worthy products and small diameter wood which will not endure strong winds and will burn at a rate three times faster than a brick home. Fire, once started, will move rapidly through these houses. They are a poor investment and a life safety issue, and everyone no matter their income or home affordability should not have to live with the higher safety risks because they can't afford a traditional home. These folks would be better off renting something they can afford or purchasing and older fixer–upper instead of throwing their money away on these types of homes.

The size of the average home in America in 1970 was approximately 1500 square feet. By 1990 that estimate had risen to approximately 2,000 square feet and now is in the neighborhood of 2,400 square feet. Every time the average young American couple (the group more susceptible to the predators), have another child they seem to be under the impression that every child must have their own bedroom. This is wonderful as long as you can afford it but most cannot. Many adults I know today grew up sharing a bedroom with a brother or sister and nobody developed lasting emotional problems from it. Rather they had to learn coping skills like how to get along with others in stressful situations. The larger a home, the costlier it is to maintain, heat, cool and the higher the taxes. These are serious things to consider when shopping for a home to purchase.

If you are a young married couple and believe that you should be entitled to every luxury that your parents took 30 years to acquire, then simply skip this chapter and I wish you the best. Granted, you are going to be truly blessed because life is really going to teach you some valuable lessons that you'll be sure to teach your children as what not to do.

The best loan on the market is the fixed interest loan, usually on a 15 year note for a home that you plan on keeping. The thirty year note will save you money if you plan on staying in the home for less than 8 years. The key, once again, in making large purchases is to pay them off as soon as possible. The longer one takes to pay something off, the more they pay the banks in interest, and remember, once again, interest is the name of the game. Compounding interest needs to be to your advantage, not the bankers. The more one pays the bank, the less one pays him or herself and that is wealth stealing, my friend. A home is a must for all of us, but the mortgage business has made home owning an extremely costly adventure. The faster one can free himself from the bondage of the house payment the faster he can become debt free the way God intended us to be. Be smart and do some serious homework before you buy your next house, and don't get strapped to the belief system of debt.

Once, the home was a place of refuge and sanctuary for families all across America. It was where we raised a family and had deep emotional ties. Unfortunately, many American's today look at their home as just an investment and once we made the home a commodity, like everything else, it no longer held the personal meaning that it used to. Know that a house is part of a neighborhood or a community and needs to be nourished and personalized. If not, it's just another piece of real estate eyeballed by the buzzards who only understand dead profit.

CHAPTER 10

THE CREDIT CARD

WARNING: The Attorney General has found that credit cards can be extremely hazardous to your fiscal health.

> *"Credit cards are the cigarettes of the fiscal world. They are extremely addictive and may cause financial cancer"* . . .
> Dave Ramsey

OK, SO THE ATTORNEY General really didn't say that, but maybe he should. The worst of the predator creditors is, without a doubt, the credit card companies. And who are the credit card companies? They are the banks. Visa, Discovery, American Express and MasterCard, etc., are bank cards. The big banks own these companies. The same guys who own the mortgage companies, the auto finance companies, the investment companies, the insurance companies, etc., etc., etc. The banksters struck gold once they understood the evolution of the credit card cash cow. The insatiable nature of the average consumer became quite clear to them by the mid to late 1980's. They understood that the general public's constant desire for stuff coupled with the convenience to purchase with plastic would assure the card companies untold wealth and profits for as long as the middle class existed.

If you remember from a previous chapter, the salary range for the average consumer has been flat since 1970 as corporate profits have sky-rocketed. This is one of the reasons credit cards, also known as revolving debt, have become so utilized because they afford the middle class with items they otherwise could not afford.

The credit card process began about 1950 when the Diner's Club card was introduced. Its purpose was to be used by travelers, mainly high-end businessmen, for the purpose of meals and entertainment. Then in 1959, American Express evolved with their card, but both of these cards worked as a closed loop system that required the card holder to pay off the full balance each month. It wasn't until the 1960's that a group of banks got together and created the Interbank Card Association, later known as MasterCard. About the same time, the Bank of America formed the BankAmericard which later became Visa. This was the beginning of the revolving debt program that we see today. This evolution has resulted in Americans being in debt to a tune of nearly one trillion dollars simply to claim the right to use someone else's money to purchase goods and services.

Once only the affluent used credit cards until the credit card industry realized that untold wealth awaited them in the vastness of the masses. By the late 1980's, credit cards became widely used by the average American. In those days, the credit card companies were all about the interest made on purchases alone. That is until a new mechanism of wealth began to appear on the horizon . . . penalties and fees. The easy use of credit cards by the 1990's lead directly to mass consumerism. Americans were buying stuff like never before thanks to plastic money. The problem was many discovered that they had over extended themselves and could no longer make those affordable monthly payments, so the credit card companies began charging penalties and fees on top of the interest to offset monies lost on those who couldn't make that monthly payment. The card companies then discovered that they could increase their corporate earnings this way and began to create policies designed to keep the average credit card holder in perpetual debt by creating a new industry within their own made out of unpaid debts. In 2008, the credit card companies hauled in over 20 billion dollars on late charges and other associated penalties alone.

Basically, it works like this. Home Depot is having a sale. So, they offer a 10 percent discount if you apply for their credit card (all credit cards are financed by a large bank someplace, regardless of what store is giving you the card). So, you need a new refrigerator because yours is eight years old, and you really want one of those trendy stainless steel ones advertised in the Home Depot flyer. You figure this is a great deal because the new coolerator is $1,000, but with your new Home Depot charge card you'll get it for only $900 once you qualify, and you most likely will qualify. Not to mention, there is no interest on the item if you pay for it in whole within one year. You can easily pay it off in a year. What a steal! You just have to make monthly payments of only $75. No problem. Then three months into the deal, your son knocks out his front tooth playing football in the front yard with the neighbor's kids. You now owe the Dentist about $2,200 because your medical insurance coverage doesn't include dental. Then, springtime rolls around and you live in north Texas where hail storms are very common. Now you have to replace the entire roof on the house after a pleasant spring shower surprised you with golf ball sized hail and your home owner's insurance deductable is $1,000. Then, your daughter has an emergency appendectomy in the fall, and you're out another $3,000 deductable to medical insurance.

Life just happened and you weren't expecting it, but the credit card company was. You haven't been able to make that easy $75 credit card payment for the last two months and the next thing you know, a year has passed and bingo! Not only are you two months late on the bill, but the interest on that new refrigerator of $247 just kicked in, not to mention your interest rate of 12 percent instantly increased to 26 percent because you defaulted on the small print in the card contract, plus the $35 a month late fee penalty for each month you couldn't make the payment will also apply. And the credit card company was counting on it. Yes, as evil as that sounds, they didn't just create a credit card for your convenience. They know that life happens to people all the time and they count on the ideology that you will completely deny that fact. They know that the middle class generally lives in debt to monthly payments and rarely budgets for those unexpected emergencies. They have studied our behavior for years and know how we think, how we live, and how we spend.

So, since you're a genius with money, you have a great idea. You can easily do a transfer to another card at 0 percent interest for the first three months. Problem is the credit card companies are a step ahead of you and see you coming. They've already installed a transfer fee with an automatic interest rate of 27 percent based on your particular risky credit history. It will kick in after 90 days and you will actually owe more on that new card than you owed on the one you couldn't pay in the first place. It's all in the small print of the contract. By the time you figure it all out, you will understand that you are the coyote holding your high interest acme credit card, and the card company is the roadrunner who sends you the bill for a lot of bird seed.

Most credit card companies do not want you to pay off your monthly bills. They want you maxed out. They can't make obscene profits on interest alone and up until February of 2010, they knew that this could double or triple their profits by entrapping the average card holder into the deep chasm of inability to pay by strapping them with extra fees and penalties. This, unfortunately, became the ideology of corporate thinking for the average credit card company. Why do you think they send out masses of credit card offers each month? They are not interested in those who can pay the balance. They're interested in those who can't. Those who pay their card balance in full each month are called "deadbeat clients" by the credit card business. Credit card companies do not make money off of people who pay their total balance each month. I am a wonderful deadbeat, and my credit card company has consistently attempted to "upgrade" my card. Unfortunately for them, I like it just the way it is. They hate me and that's ok. No love loss here. The point is, be careful if you ever upgrade your card, especially if you have a cash back contract because once you upgrade, you run the risk of losing your cash back deal. Remember it's all in the fine print of the contract.

The average American household is in debt to credit cards on the average of approximately $9,000, and most can only make the minimum monthly payment. If you attempted to pay off your credit card bill by making those easy minimum payments, it would take you approximately 18 years, and you would pay nearly 1/3 of that in interest. That is if you don't make another purchase on the card. More people are using credit cards today than ever before and for minor purchases without a clue of the cost of using someone else's money.

Many years ago, I could not pay my credit card payment, yet I was still getting credit card applications from the same company in the mail. As a matter-of-fact, credit card companies know what they are doing and that it works well for them. The average American receives at least two credit card applications in the mail each week. That equates to 102 credit card applications a year for each adult over the age of 21 in the United States alone. That is over 300 million credit card applications mailed annually in our country. The cost of bulk mail alone could feed a third world nation for months. Visa has approximately 180 million customers in the United States while MasterCard has approximately 165 million, so you can simply imagine the money made by the banks on these two cards alone.

Why would credit card companies take such a risk on people who may default on their cards? Because it works! Americans are infatuated with spending and comfort, and the convenience of purchase by plastic will assure the banks with a steady stream of cash from a middle class that knows no better and will feel further comforted by making those easy minimum payments. Most credit card companies want them as financial slaves for life. They even target those who have filed for bankruptcy. Why? Because those people have already proven to be bad at personal finances and as of 2006, the bankruptcy laws in the US changed in favor of the credit card companies. Those banksters lobbied well in order to clamp down on those who would not pay their credit card bills and Congress agreed. Now credit card payments along with interest and fees cannot be excluded in the default of a bankruptcy and must be paid. In several cases, those who file for bankruptcy prove to make the same financial mistakes over and over, and this is good for the card companies.

Once people default on a card, the credit card company will do everything within their legal power to obtain payment. Once all else fails, they will most likely sell that bad debt to a debt collection agency for pennies on the dollar. This is when things usually get ugly for the defaulting credit card holder. Many debt collection companies are owned and operated by unscrupulous and unethical people who will stop at nothing to collect what you owe. These people are very good at what they do and will bend and break the law to accomplish their objective. They have been known to threaten people with arrests, garnishments, and repossession of properties and even jail. They have contacted family members, employers, friends, neighbors, associates and clients and harassed people all in the attempt to get their hands on what you owe and legally, once your credit card goes to collections, you owe them. They just have to abide by the Fair Debt Collections Practice Act but most do not, and they will harass you till the day you die. So, the best way to deal with such risk is to simply pay what you owe to the credit card company in the first place and avoid the hassle.

Americans are consumers, plain and simple. The average credit card holder in America has three to four major credit cards, and most only make the minimum monthly payments and are paying interest and fees just for the convenience of using the credit card. College students are carrying more and more debt on credit cards with the average student indebted three to seven thousand dollars. 15 percent of Americans are consistently late on their card payments. 26 to 30 percent of Americans do not pay their bills on time, and most pay the credit card bills last. Credit card defaults in 2009 reached near 100 billion dollars, four times that of 2007. 185 million Americans have at least one credit card, and only one third of those can make the full monthly payment.

To make matters worse, the average person has very little say so in the credit card contract. Credit card companies make all the rules and few, if any, are in the favor of the consumer. 78 percent of credit card companies immediately raise interest rates once one payment is late. The companies can arbitrarily change the rules of the contract at any time. Up until 2010, they could raise your interest rate if you show any credit risks with any other debt as well, even though you were making regular payments to them without any problems. Once they could find any indicator that listed you as a risky customer, up went your rate which could be devastating if you owed several thousands of dollars and legally, there was nothing you could do about it. In most states, there is really no limit to how high they can raise the interest on a card.

The bank's objective is to obtain customers with revolving debt because traditionally, these customers never get out of debt and that means continuous profit for the card companies. Many people get so far in debt with a card that they find themselves paying 75 percent each month to fees and penalties, so they do a balance transfer to another card with a low introductory rate which will soon skyrocket to 17 percent. The next thing you know, they can't make that payment either so they are hit with a default rate of 27 percent. So, they look for another introductory rate at a low interest and do another transfer and the whole process starts all over again. There is no way out of this nightmare.

Fortunately, in 2009, the Obama administration finally took action against the credit card companies when the President signed the Credit Card Accountability, Responsibility and Disclosure Act (CARD) into law. This is the first step the US government has taken against the big banks in order to protect consumers since the 1970's.

The Act changes the way that credit card companies do business. No longer can they raise your interest rate without letting you know, nor can they send you a bill without a 21 day pay cycle. They can no longer raise your interest by considering you a high risk card holder if you default on another bill, and they can no longer target college students.

Until the Act, credit card companies began to really go after college students knowing that the ages of 18 to 25 were known to quickly go into debt and most would default which would mean penalties and fees into the millions . . . cha ching! Many companies were known to pay college administrative boards upwards to $100,000 for the right to set up a table at the college book store during times of registration. A sure bet with unsuspecting college kids was the T-shirt with the college emblem or mascot on front as a free gift just for filling out an application for their card. The key was to sign up as many life-long card users as possible, because many college kids are not responsible enough to pay the balance each month and quickly join the ranks of those strapped to fees and penalties. But somebody has to pay for beer and pizza sooner or later. The burden was on the kids and many were graduating college with a bachelor's degree that had little or no value strapped with college loan debt, as well as credit card debt and most had no job and no prospects for one. Unfortunately, several suicides of college kids have been reported over the last ten years because these kids were bullied by debt collectors after they had maneuvered themselves into mountains debt.

The CARD Act has placed new restrictions on credit card companies by not allowing them within 100 feet of a college campus. The Act even restricted card holders to the age of 21 before one can even apply for a credit card. This is the best part of the Act as it keeps the predators away from those most likely to fall into the snare of the trap.

The Act does take several steps to protect consumers, but the credit card companies are already finding ways around many of the obstacles. Some argue that the new laws will hurt those consumers who do pay their balances off each month as credit card companies have raised interest rates and created new fees that punish the responsible card users to make up for the losses for those cardholders who default. The credit card industry claims that the new laws have resulted in the loss of over 15 billion dollars for the banksters. That is a lot of bonus money, and the banks have big-time attorneys that are going to help them get around many of those laws in order that those bonus checks for the guys at the top keep coming in.

Remember who owns the credit card companies: the big banks. The same guys the government rescued. The law isn't designed to put the card companies out of business and leaves room for loopholes that the credit card companies will surely take advantage of. The end game is the companies will not suffer and will pass on most of their losses to the consumer because that is their nature. Snakes bite! It is their nature. You can't have a rattlesnake as a pet. Sooner or later he will bite you. Why? Because it is in his very nature! It is what snakes do. It is in the nature of credit card companies to think of ways to increase their bottom line regardless of ethics, and nobody, including the US government is going to stop that.

We live in a free market system. Unfortunately with any free system of trade, someone is going to attempt to sell snake oil. Government intervention, though well intended, most often hurts the very group it attempts to protect. If you are not wise to the snake oil game, you can easily become another victim of their scam. The bottom line is the best consumer is a wise consumer. It is your responsibility to pay for what you purchase and live within your means. The best way to do that is with good ole cash! You cannot over-extend cash. Once it's gone it's gone and you can no longer purchase something you can't afford. You will also not pay more than the item is worth as you are doing by using plastic. The average person spends 17 percent more when buying with credit cards than with cash because there is a psychological aspect to spending with cash that doesn't exist while using credit cards.

No one can steal your identity when paying with cash either and if your wallet is stolen, the only thing they can spend is the cash that's in it. Another good reason for buying with cash is it will remind you to stay within your means. If you can't afford it, don't buy it. Debt is a poor man's way of getting what he can't afford by using someone else's money that must be paid back. The credit card companies love the poor man.

Remember, using credit cards is simply buying stuff with someone else's money, and they are going to want their money back plus interest. Using a credit card and paying the entire balance monthly takes discipline. If you use a card, you must pay it off each and every month in full or else you will be a slave to the banksters and continue to make them richer. Do not live beyond your means because life is going to happen and unexpected expenses are guaranteed. You can quickly find yourself unable to make that payment and begin to make only the minimum and the entrapment will begin. Be smart and know what the credit card companies are about and how you fit into their schemes.

Regardless of the nature of the credit card companies, nobody is responsible for your debt except you. You have to pay for anything you purchase and if you are deep in debt to credit card companies, stop using the card and call the company to see what you can do to settle the debt or set up a payment schedule that works for you. No one can help you eliminate your debt, no matter how much they advertise that they can. You can work with your creditors yourself buy picking up the phone and facing your demons. It makes no sense to pay someone to help you pay off what you owe.

Use a check or debit card to purchase items such as groceries, gas, eating out, etc. Don't worry if the people in line behind you have to wait for you to write the check; they don't have to pay your bills. A debit card can do anything a credit card can do and if you think you must have a credit card, just keep one. Remember the average person carries at least four credit cards. Don't be average. You only need one and pay it off every single month. And be aware that bank cards carry an average of 12 percent interest where store cards carry upwards to 21 to 28 percent. Cut up and rid yourself of store cards and gas cards. You do not need them. Every major chain will ask you if you will be interested in saving 10 percent by applying for their card once you go to pay for a large purchase. Forget the 10 percent. Don't do it!

Credit cards work for those who are responsible, but it takes great discipline in today's culture of self indulgence to be responsible. Advertisers, marketers, and scammers are everywhere trying to convince you to use their product, and credit card companies are no different. They are all about interest, penalties and fees. That is the name of the game. That interest is better made by you by using cash to purchase only the things you need. Staying out of debt is becoming almost impossible for most Americans who continue to live beyond their means. Be wise and rid yourself of the plastic. Use cash and put that interest to use for you like the fiscal responsible people do.

CHAPTER 11

TAXES

JUST THE WORD "TAX" can leave horrible impressions on a guy. Taxes backwards spells "Satan." Or at least it should! Today we see all kinds of taxes. Income tax, state tax, gasoline tax, inheritance tax, school tax, city tax, social security tax, property tax, sales tax, import & export tax, telephone tax, transportation tax, bridge tax, toll tax, poll tax, road tax, hotel tax, luxury tax, sin tax, county tax, hospital tax, tax, tax, and more tax.

Taxes are nothing new and can be found as far back as governments existed. Even Jesus was taxed by the Roman government who perfected the over-burdening tax system on the Roman citizenry. It was found by the rulers of Rome that taxes had to be levied in order to pay for vast armies in the beginning, but the more the Roman government did for the empire the more expensive things were to maintain. The solution was to tax more and more from the vast empire which was one of the reasons Rome fell. The New Testament even explains how the tax collector was one of the lowest reputed individuals in that society and most despised.

Immorality is expensive! Big governments are immoral by Christian standards. The more immoral a culture becomes, the more expensive it is to keep. The more the government takes care of individual needs, the less convicted and independent its citizens become resulting in higher taxation.

Taxes in America began long before the revolutionary war when King George III of England laid heavy tax burdens down on the colonies to help finance England's world conquest and to pay for the Hessen soldiers he was renting from Prince William consequently keeping the colonies in line. One of the 24 articles of concern the colonies levied against the King was "taxation without representation." Many believe this was the reason for the American Revolution, but actually it was number 17 on the list but never-the-less was a huge motivator for the colonies to go to war against the most powerful country in the world.

Once the revolution was over and the smoke cleared, the new colonial government had to have some kind of income to support a national infrastructure. Enter the sin tax, as taxes were levied on mainly items such as whisky, tobacco and other various creature comforts. But the Constitution forbid a personal income tax on the general populace, and by 1812 the government had repealed most all taxes. The small government basically existed on standard tariffs and excise taxes for various items of ownership.

Then the Civil War came along and President Lincoln was forced to create a type of Federal Income Tax to help pay for the cost of the war, but it was repealed by Congress as unconstitutional by 1872. But governments have to have some kind of money to support a nation. A standing army is a must which to protect a country against foreign invaders, and there must be law enforcement and other services to protect and serve the general public. Then with the advent of automobiles and the industrial age, the government began to expand and more funds were needed. In 1909, a congressman introduced a bill that would change the face of the US government forever. That bill was ratified into law via the 16th Amendment in 1913, since that time, taxation has become an addicting drug for federal, state and local governments who can't seem to get enough of our income.

The tax wasn't much at first and was really designed only for the wealthy. A 1% tax was levied on anyone making over $3,000 annually with a 6% tax on anyone making over $500,000. And as it goes with the federal government, once a tax is in place, like cancer it grows as more taxes are needed to sustain ever-growing governmental programs consistently introduced by Congress through special interests. Then in 1935 during the Great Depression, President Roosevelt, as part of the New Deal, created the social security tax program designed to help aging Americans subsidize their retirement years. This would have been a great source of income for our elderly, but Congress has robbed the system blind. Every President since JFK has signed some kind of bill using Social Security monies as funding. Then, more and more government jobs had to be created to handle the growth of the nation's needs as Americans became less and less independent. Also in 1942, FDR signed into law a bill that created tax on payroll and quarterly income. This tax applied to 2/3 of the nation as the no tax ideology of our forefather's began to erode.

Medicare, Social Security, infrastructures, highways, street signs, telecommunications, national defense, national park programs, research programs, national health programs, housing programs, food stamps, prisons, electrical power, space programs, mental health programs, and various other governmental pork entities began requiring consistent funding. A fine example is the temporary US Department of Energy created during the Carter Administration to help America stop our dependence on foreign oil. Today that department still exists with over 140,000 employees and contractors, though its mission has been changed several times since its inception. State, county and municipal taxes have risen dramatically, too, with taxes for infrastructure, fire, police, municipal services, bridges, roads, and more and more social programs designed to help the poor, (the largest growing group in America today) which has dramatically increased in the last ten years. Taxes for local school districts typically make up approximately 50% of all local taxation. Then the federal government is paying billions to pay back interest on loans from foreign investors through the Federal Reserve Bank to print tons of money annually. This is paid with tax dollars (approximately 20 billion a year). On top of that, more government jobs have been created to handle the growth of the nation's needs as Americans become more and more dependent on Uncle Sam.

And what about those sin taxes? Those levied upon non-essential commodities such as beer, wine, spirits, tobacco, gambling, etc. Actually, those have been around since the dawn of taxation usually as some kind of excise. Today, this is the government's go-to tax. These are items that our society usually believes are sinful or vice and should be taxed out of existence but never are. Why? Because they bring in billions of dollars a year for local, state and the federal governments! A pack of cigarettes in New York City will now cost approximately $9.30 with $5.22 going to tax. New York is the costliest city in America for smokers, and the state of New York one of the heaviest taxed. And in all states, a tax on liquor, beer and wine in the name of licensure and certifications brings in billions of dollars annually. And what about gambling? The government loves gamblers, especially those who win the mega-millions Lotto. The tax man will be the first person they meet at the Lotto office once they arrive to collect their winnings. Uncle Sam takes his cut first.

Besides, people are not going to give up pleasurable items, no matter how sinful or dangerous they are. Our nature is to be drawn to such things and without that moral compass that we saw in years past, those items will always be in growing demand. This is why we have a 400 billion dollar a year illegal drug trade in the United States.

The US Tax Code is now over 7 million words long printed 60 lines per page. Americans spend over 200 billion dollars annually complying with income tax requirements of more than 21 megabytes in length. This mega-document fills more than 16,000 letter sized pages, and the IRS sends out approximately 8 billion pages of forms and instructions annually. Nearly 300,000 trees a year are cut down to produce the amount of paper required for IRS forms and instructions. The IRS employs approximately 114,000 people, twice as many as the CIA and five times that of the FBI. 60 percent of tax payers must hire professional tax consultants and CPAs to complete their taxes each year. There are at least 480 different tax forms, each with numerous pages of easy-to-use instructions. One of the most used and easiest forms is the 1040E which comes with 33 pages of "how to."

There really is no exact number of pages for the tax code because it is constantly changing. Each year the IRS has to deal with loopholes that must be closed or created and tax items that must be changed for various political or fiscal reasons. It is not uncommon for the federal government to change tax laws in order to assist some failing industry or promote a living standard via federal programs. One example is the interest savings homeowners receive on their annual home mortgages. Renters do not see this break because it is designed to encourage Americans to own their own homes. Other savings designed by the feds are the child income credits which offer a savings in annual taxes of $500 per child per household as long as they are under the age of 18.

According to consulting firm Deboitte Tax, a family with four children under the age of 17, making a combined income of less than $60,000 annually will pay virtually no Federal income tax. Almost 1/3 of the country can qualify for this situation. This, of course, does not exempt those families from all other taxes. The truth is the average American taxpayer pays approximately 13 percent of their income to Uncle Sam through federal income taxes. The bottom 50 percent of American earners pay only 2.99 percent of income taxes. The top 1 percent of earners pay approximately 39.89 percent. The top 5 percent of earners pay 60.14 percent, and the top 10 percent of earners pay 70.79 percent according to figures kept by the IRS. The lowest earning workers, especially those with dependents, pay very little to no federal income taxes as a group and actually get a small subsidy from the federal government when they apply child credits and earned income credits.

In 2010, to add insult to injury, 2.4 million undocumented people in America collected 4.2 billion dollars in earned income credits from Uncle Sam (that means you).

But none of us will escape the full brunt of total taxation. As a matter-of-fact, Americans are taxed to the tune of 1/3 of their annual incomes once all taxation is finalled. Sales tax, county, state, federal, etc., will cost each American dearly. And with a comprehensive nationwide health plan in our future, those taxes will increase remarkably in the next four years and will affect the poorest the most. If you remember back in an earlier chapter, I explained where your life income is going and that 1/3 will go to taxes. In 1913, when this mess began, Uncle Sam was a younger and fit fellow who has become extremely obese and now must have a daily portion of your hard earned dollar to survive. Uncle Sam is addicted to your earnings. You can blame the IRS if you like, you can blame the federal government, the liberals or conservatives, the rich or the poor, you can even blame George Bush, but year after year Americans have voted people into office who have created these taxes because the bottom line is . . . the more power we give to the government to insure our needs are met, the more it will cost us. Freedom the way our forefathers designed it did not include the government taking over the auto business, the banking business, the housing industry and healthcare. All of that is expensive and the more the government takes control, the more it is going to cost you and me. So prepare yourselves for more government entitlement programs and continued excessive government spending.

The only hope you have is to move your savings to offshore accounts that are exempt from US governmental taxation, but the government is already working on ways to stop that. The other and most productive way for the average working class American is to deposit savings in tax free savings programs or deferred retirement accounts, but even those will be taxed once you go to use them in your retirement years. At least you won't be taxed as much.

Once many years ago, I knew a young woman who truly believed that each American should feel obligated to give at least half of his or her income to the US government for the privilege of living in such a wonderful country. Can you imagine that anyone in this country could have such a completely misguided outlook? Actually, there are many throughout the world that do and we have historically referred to them as socialists, communist or hardcore radical leftists. There are many in our nation today who think just like her and unfortunately, they have taken charge of our government over the last few years. Your only hope is to vote. God only requires a 10 percent tax on his church through tithing. The federal government, who believes its mission is ultimately more important, imposes much more than the creator of the universe. Ironic indeed for a country who originally shed thousands of American lives so that their ancestors would never live in an over-taxed culture.

Our nation must have a tax system to exist. Justice Oliver Wendell Holmes remarked, *"Taxes are what we pay for a civilized society,"* which is true to a certain extent! However, once taxes move from what is necessary for a proper government to over-taxation of the populace, then, it becomes tax tyranny. Chief Justice John Marshal was quoted saying, *"Those with the power to tax also have the power to destroy."* When our politicians continue to single out members of one specific group in order to buy votes from a majority of others by promising those others that the former will pay a disproportionate amount of taxes is a form of tyranny. Taking more and more control of free enterprises, healthcare, businesses, and mandating overloaded tax laws upon the citizenry is another form of tyranny.

High tax rates discourage people from working, saving and investing resulting in fewer jobs and slower growth. It also encourages people in states or districts with high tax rates to look elsewhere.

Currently, the U.S. corporate tax rate is 39.3 percent, the highest in the industrial world. Corporate CEOs are not going to take a bite out of their personal earnings and bonuses and will happily move a company to Mexico to keep from paying high taxes. The problem is the working class or middle class worker gets squeezed between greedy government taxers and greedy corporate CEOs virtually leaving folks like you and me out in the cold.

Currently, our tax system penalizes work and productivity with high tax rates. Then there seems to be a governmental bias against saving and investing and if some in congress had their way, interest made on 401ks would be taxed annually as well once they mature. If you place your earned dollar into a savings account you are taxed on any interest made from that money which you already paid taxes on when you earned it. The current tax system also has unfair loopholes created by lobbyists who represent the top 10 percent of earners. And lastly, the current system requires a very aggressive IRS. The U.S. government places high priority on tax collection. You can commit all kinds of serious crimes against people in the U.S., and you are considered innocent until proven guilty. This doesn't seem to apply with the IRS. If you owe Uncle Sam, you better pay. Besides, it is our duty as Christians to suffer, even under the guise of the government. Jesus said, "Give unto Caesar that which is Caesar's, but give unto God that which is God's." Not paying your taxes is as wrong as being over-taxed.

There is a growing amount of people, politicians included, who are suggesting and even demanding that we repeal the 16th amendment and do away with the current tax code. Most of these people suggest a flat 10 percent tax on every working American based on earned or received income. If a person makes $10,000 annually, he will pay no more than $1,000 in taxes, and if he makes 10 million annually, he will pay no more than 1 million in taxes. Many wealthy proponents argue this would devalue a need for loopholes and would not be fair to the top majority of money earners while others argue that $1,000 is way too much for a person who only makes $10,000 annually but for the majority, this tax makes more than perfect sense.

Another option is a national sales tax. Meaning, you would only pay taxes on items you purchase. This would be a very fair system for all but would not have a method that would require a tax break for the poor, and the wealthy would make out like bandits. The other problem would be Congress's insatiable desire to go after these sales taxes over a period of time by increasing them to the point that we would be right back in the same boat with an over bloated tax system.

And if all that isn't enough to be concerned with, there is a new taxing beast emerging from the darkest pits of hell. The world court or UN, whichever one wishes to call this over bureaucratic system of world dominators, is the latest in line with their hand out. The latest "world summit" meeting saw an overwhelming desire of world leaders appeasing the UN by agreeing that top performing countries should be taxed in the neighborhood of approximately 20 billion dollars a year beginning in 2012 in order to assist developing countries. Helping developing countries is a great idea, but not at the cost of raking sovereign nations with overburdening tax systems to do it. And it doesn't take anything more than a "presidential agreement" to commit the United States into some kind of long term tax commitment to a corrupt world system which would in turn affect our sovereignty as a nation and chip away at our Constitution and our personal freedoms. In the long run, we will see more and more UN attempts to set up a world-wide government that would destroy our bill of rights and enslave Americans into the arena of world court domination.

And lastly, if you've ever wondered just what your tax dollars are going to pay for, here is an eye-opening list which may surprise you. The list was posted as a Yahoo News Exclusive dated April 15, 2011, and composed by writer Jane Sasseen. The list is the percentage of tax based on those collected from an average American family of four who, with deductions totaled, pay approximately 10 to 15 percent of earned income to Uncle Sam. Here is where those tax dollars go.

Social Security	20.4%
Defense	20.2%
Medicare	13.1%
Low Income Assistance	9.3%
Net Interest Payment	6.6%
Unemployment Compensation	4.7%
Veteran's Affairs	3.1%
Education	2.9%
Law Enforcement/Homeland Security	2.4%
Transportation	2.3%
Federal Employees & Buildings	1.4%
Env. Protection/Natural Resources	1.0%
Space & Science	0.7%
Agriculture	0.7%
Housing & Community Development	0.6%
Social Services	0.6%
Foreign Aid	0.6%
Workplace & Safety Rights	0.5%
Diplomacy and Embassies	0.4%
IRS	0.4%
Statistics & Weather	0.3%
Telecommunications	0.3%
Trade & Economic Development	0.3%
Native Americans	0.2%
Congress	0.2%
Post Office	0.1%
Arts & Culture	0.1%

I think we would all agree, sales tax, flat tax or world tax . . . something has to change. The current system cannot continue as is.

But allow me to make it clear. Our government is but a reflection of who we are. Americans have developed very poor voting habits. We have become obese and lazy and have allowed the government to take over many institutions that were once untouchable by the feds. As long as we continue to allow or expect the federal government to take care of us, the higher our taxes will rise. We are the land of the free and the brave. Freedom is scary, true freedom that is, and it takes the brave to face it daily. Are you brave enough to be free, or would you rather the government do it all for you? And one thing is absolutely sure: your government will never have enough of your money and will always need more.

CHAPTER 12

THE LOTTERY

"IF THE LOTTERY WAS a money making tool, the rich would be lined up at convenience stores across the nation," says Dave Ramsey. This is one item that more people, mostly poor and financially ignorant, throw more money at than any other. The idea of suddenly walking into millions appeals to most people who cannot manage money. Not only is the lottery a tax on the poor as mentioned by many financial analysts, but it robs them weekly of money they could be building wealth with. Unfortunately, most of these folks do not have the mindset of saving but are mostly ignorant of how money works, and they are under the false belief that winning the lottery is going to be the end-all of life's problems. If you can't manage it before you get it, you won't manage it once you have it and will most likely end up worse than you were when you were simply broke. The bigger the money, the bigger the problems, and most people are not equipped emotionally or spiritually to deal with the problems that the big bucks bring into their lives.

In 2011, over 70 billion dollars was spent on lottery tickets in the United States. Only 39 billion was paid out in winnings. The lottery promises a life of dreams come true with just a ticket and a little luck, but experts and some past lottery winners tell a different story.

Winning the lottery can turn your dreams into nightmares. Just when someone wins that untold amount of wealth and thinks all his problems are over, a whole new set of problems arises and many far outweigh anything these people have ever dealt with before. Take the man from West Virginia who won a whopping 314 million dollars in a mega-millions jackpot on Christmas day in 2002. Already the owner of a successful company, one would think he would have had more sense than he did. After taking a cash payout of $111 million his life and his behavior took a rapid turn for the worst. More than $500,000 in cash and cashier's checks were stolen out of his SUV while it was parked outside a strip club called the "Pink Pony."

Later, another $100,000 was stolen from his car parked just outside his house. Then he was arrested several times on assault charges, and the friend of his granddaughter was found dead in his house, the victim of a drug overdose. After two drunk-driving charges, he was ordered to a rehab center by a district judge. And nearly two years to the day, his 17 year old granddaughter was found dead of a drug overdose. He was known to give her a $4,000 a week allowance. He has since faced several lawsuits and is now bankrupt.

Then there is the man from Pennsylvania who won $16.2 million and now lives on a Social Security check of $450 a month after mooching relatives and a greedy girlfriend broke him. How about the woman who won the New Jersey lottery not once but twice for a total of $5.4 million? She now lives in a small mobile home and survives on Social Security, too. She put most of her winnings back into the gambling racket through slot machines. A man from Texas won a 37 million dollar lotto, but his spending habits pushed his wife away and his life spiraled out of control. He committed suicide two years after his big win. England's youngest lotto winner ever was a sixteen year old girl who won millions only to blow it all on drugs and friends by the time she was 22. She is now a single mother, dead broke, living in a friend's apartment and has attempted suicide twice. And there are many more stories just like these which include drug and alcohol abuse, massive infidelity, separated families and siblings, hostilities and even murder. What is believed to be a ticket to the good life can easily turn into a life of debt, divorce, addiction and jail.

Many Lotto winners, especially those who win small jackpots, disappointingly discover that they aren't the millionaire they thought they were once Uncle Sam is finished with them. Then they find out that many winnings are set up on a weekly or monthly schedule that only pays out approximately $50,000 to $100,000 a year for twenty years but they go out and buy luxury items because they believe in their minds that they are millionaires. Then most of these folks purchase that big dream house without the understanding that maintaining a mansion costs a lot of money. Most never consider the cost of upkeep, higher utility bills, insurance and taxes, and soon find themselves severely over extended.

Tales of sudden riches is nothing new, and horror stories of instant cash millionaires are more common than we Americans wish to believe. Winning the lottery is so ingrained in our pop culture reports Susan Bradley, founder of the Sudden Money Institute, an organization set up to advise the "suddenly rich" that all the warnings in the world won't stop the poor from playing the Lotto. In our culture, so many believe that money is a good thing and that more is better. People can witness the carnage that instant money has brought to the lives of so many but believe that they would fare much better if a pile of cash instantly came their way. Everyone thinks that winning the lottery is a problem they would like to have. Many who come into the winnings suddenly think they now have a life with no rules or boundaries and end up alienating those closest to them. Many others find that they are harassed daily by friends, family and acquaintances looking for a handout, and once the telemarketers and other panhandlers know where they are, they find themselves living in a camera protected compound suffering from paranoia not knowing who they can trust.

But the lottery is big business in the United States with Americans spending over $25 billion annually on that scratch-off chance to live the easy life. Many Lotto programs claim that the Lotto helps lower taxes in certain states by subsidizing property taxes in poor neighborhoods, but in truth it's the poor who are purchasing the vast majority of the lotto tickets. 82 percent of Lotto sales occur in poor neighborhoods and communities. This is why many experts call the Lotto a tax on the poor. Many others claim that the lottery helps subsidize education by transferring millions into state education systems. If that were true, we wouldn't be paying on average 50 percent of our total county taxes for local school or state education taxes.

Gambling is never a good way to secure wealth and worse, it can become addictive. Many have been known to lose their entire livelihoods because of gambling addictions. And we've all heard the story of the guy who went to Vegas and immediately won the jackpot on the slot machine. In most cases, he turned right around and put it all right back in. The fact is, the house always wins, and if you do not understand that then you are most likely going to live a life filled with disappointment. I have been to casinos full of cigarette smoking grandmothers spending all their Social Security checks on false hopes of winning that lucky slot, then go home to their small mobile homes or apartments with nothing to show but another frozen dinner while watching Wheel of Fortune.

Billions and billions of dollars are handed over to state gaming commissions, casinos and lottery commissions annually instead of being placed into savings accounts. The average serious Lotto ticket buyer will spend at minimum, $50 a week or more playing the lotto or purchasing Lottery scratch offs. That adds up to $2,600 annually. Take that and place it in a mutual fund each year for 20 years gaining compound interest (which is what mutual funds do) and that would equate to $83,180 and that's a small investment earning a low 4 percent interest. That is how the wealthy play the lottery.

I frequent a local convenient store in town where I purchase gas. It is a huge lottery store and just above the counter are large pictures of the recent Lotto winners holding up their winnings with huge smiles on their faces as if they have cheated fate. Truth be known, the fellow holding the $8,000 winning check most likely spent over $26,000 in the last ten years to finally win. And many avid Lotto winners do win, but their winnings never, if ever, out score what they have paid for lottery tickets in their lifetime. For every one Lotto winner at the convenience store counter, there is a trash bin in the back full of tickets that lost. Any fiscally intelligent person knows that the house always wins.

The lure of easy money has always fascinated those who have no fiscal discipline or fiscal understanding. It always will, and as P.T. Barnum exclaimed, "There's a sucker born every minute," and he should have known because he sold more snake oil than most. There are financial predators everywhere, and they all use our own greed against us in order to lure us into their trap. That is exactly what the Lotto does. If you're one of those who share the idea that "somebody's got to win," then good luck and I hope you find your pot of gold, but for 98 percent of those who go hunting, all they find for their trouble is more trouble. Be smart and don't take the gamble that could take your wealth. Investing over time is the only sure thing you have.

CHAPTER 13

ADVANCED CASH
AND PREDATORY LENDERS

IN 2009, A PHILADELPHIA woman discovered that she had a roof leak in her suburban home. A professional roofer advised her that her home needed a new roof which would cost about $6,000. She went to her bank for a loan using her paid-off home as equity. Unfortunately, a slick talking loan officer convinced her that she should get an entire remodel of the kitchen with a total home improvement loan. She unwittingly took the bait and now, after a hidden pre-payment loan clause and a sliding interest rate that matured from 9 percent to 23.8 percent, she is $80,000 in debt on a home she once owned outright. And though this banker should be in jail for fraud, it was all perfectly legal.

Unfortunately, there is a predatory or sub-prime lending market out there which targets primarily female, low income, elderly and minority groups of low to middle income families whose incomes lag behind the typical two parent income. Many of these unscrupulous rascals are good at introducing one type of loan but encouraging another by convincing the would-be homeowner not to worry about the small print.

Many people lost their homes in the collapse of the sub-prime market because of mortgage companies that behaved like thieves and con artists using sleight of hand to incorporate their schemes instead of honest traditional practices that protected future homeowners. Even still, after the crash we continue to see some less than honest practices such as "Equity Stripping" where a loan officer encourages the homeowner to borrow against their equity such as seen in the story above. Or "Loan Flipping" where the lender encourages the home owner to refinance after refinance with huge fees added each time, or "Loan Packing" where the lender adds charges which the borrower didn't need or ask for such as certain kinds of unnecessary insurance all the while adding more into the monthly payment plan via interest to be paid back over years.

Other predatory practices include bill consolidation equity loans encouraging the consumer to pay off credit card, retail, and motor vehicle debt by consolidating them all into one home loan promising lower monthly payments. While lower monthly payments do result from this transaction, the consumer trades short-term debt for long-term. Instead of paying off their bills in three to four years, it will now take them 15 to 30 years. The unbeknownst consumer will also pay much more in interest over the life of the loan.

Then, there is the unscrupulous balloon note. A predatory lender reduces the monthly payment on a home loan by having the borrower pay off only the accrued interest each month. This sounds good to the unsuspecting homeowner living on a budget as it gives the impression that the homeowner will have more cash each month, and he will for a little while unsuspecting the nightmare just around the corner. This kind of financing will result in huge balloon payments at the end of the repayment term, usually ranging from 10 to 15 years. The borrower often believes he is paying down the loan and is completely unaware of the balloon payment due at the end of the term. The borrower may owe as much at the end of the term as they originally borrowed. Elderly borrowers are often unable to refinance the loan making foreclosure inevitable.

Payday lenders are another form of the underbelly of financial institutions. These rascals prey on working consumers who generally live paycheck-to-paycheck offering loans of as much as $1,000 against a future payroll or government benefit check. Typically, the consumer writes a check for $230 to borrow $200 for two weeks (usually their next payday). The actual cost of that loan for two weeks is $30, or an annual percentage rate (APR) of 390 percent. Some payday loans can end up costing consumers more than 900 percent.

Proponents in the business say their practice offers cash-strapped consumers help in emergency situations. But these folks because of their lack of financial savvy are typically strapped for cash consistently, and the proponents ignore the fact that far too many people get trapped into a vicious cycle of loan after loan. Payday loans almost always create more financial burdens for consumers than they solve. These lenders act more like drug dealers whose best customers are the hopelessly addicted. They love desperation and ignorance as it brings them profits of joy over the entrapment of the unaware.

Consumers desperate enough to visit a payday lender often find there's not enough money on payday to cover the loan and all the fees, and still make rent or put food on the table. No problem. The payday lender is happy to "roll it over" for a new fee, leaving the borrower owing most or all of the $230 at the end of the next transaction. That brings the total finance charges for a $200 one month loan to $60. That is exactly what the payday lender is counting on. Rarely is this a one-time transaction, and borrowers typically make ten to twelve such transactions before they finally figure out their mistake.

These types of financial entrapments are becoming more and more regulated in most states under industry-friendly rules adopted by state finance commissions and federal banking regulators as well as state representatives as they attempt to rein these rascals in. In many states, these lenders are now using unregulated Credit

Service Organization status as a way to evade new federal guidelines. Fortunately, the future for these guys looks gloomy as more and more states are introducing laws and regulatory practices designed to put them completely out of business.

These types of bankers and lenders just go to show that donning a new suit and getting a nice haircut doesn't make a career criminal a respectable businessman. Every reader needs to desperately understand the importance of identifying predators when they see them. Most people who get strapped for cash to the point that they would utilize these rascals just do not have a clue of the real cost of dealing with the devil. Avoid these people at all costs even if that means going without a meal for 24 hours. There is nothing that would require the need for their dirty money.

Other practices that take advantage of the poor and financially ignorant are rent-to-own businesses. Most of these businesses usually rent TV's, appliances, furniture, jewelry and computers to unsuspecting customers with the option to buy. Most of their customers are young consumers who don't have a clue what they're up against or people who have very bad credit to the point they can't purchase consumer items any other way. And the rent-to-owners know it.

It is typical for someone to walk into a rent-to-own store looking for a TV. The rent-to-own store is happy to oblige the pigeon with a great affordable deal on a brand new big screen TV for what appears to be a very low weekly charge for 72 weeks, and they'll even deliver for free. And as long as the pigeon is in the shop, might as well look around as a computer can be had for another cheap affordable payment for another 72 weeks. Once 72 weeks has passed, the happy TV renter now owns that big screen TV and computer, and it was so easy. What he now realizes is the real cost of the items which with interest added at 220 percent was five times more than he could have purchased it at a legitimate retailer.

It is typical for a rent to own store to purchase a TV for $1100 and rent to own it for well over $6,000. This is the nature of their game, and proponents of the business claim they provide a leasing business not a rental business. They also have a history of ignoring fair consumer laws and acts as they consistently rip off the general public. Be very cautious of many furniture and appliance stores who finance their own products. Some in the business scam unsuspecting buyers into outrageous deals designed to rip them off with exceedingly high interest rates. If they are advertising an outrageous deal that looks too good to be true, it is because it IS too good to be true and a scam exists in the fine print. Buyer, always beware of what's in the fine print.

Unfortunately, there are no WANTED posters for some of these folks, but there should be. They tend to place their stores in low income communities and prey off of the desperation of the poor and fiscal illiterates. It is our responsibility as consumers to understand how these people do business and that they will steal from us if given the slightest chance. Your ignorance is their strength, and they will see you coming a mile away if you are not up to speed on their game. They are predators. It may be best to do without than to purchase goods this way.

CHAPTER 14

HEALTH CARE

THE BEST EXAMPLE OF our current Godless business model is found in the health care industry. Our lack of virtue in commerce is best expressed in a system that has come to justify the very practice of thievery in which so many over the ages have hung by the neck for their part in its vice. This industry makes millions at the devilish art of taking advantage of the sick and the dying and not many are exempt from the talons of its demonic grip.

There is one very important rule that every single American should know and that is anytime the government gets involved in private business practices, it can be guaranteed that prices in that industry can be expected to sky-rocket. The advent of Medicare and Medicaid coupled with modern corporate business practices and the high cost of pharmaceuticals which lack the guidance of Christian morals and ethics has created one of the greatest burdens upon Americans since the illegal and outrageous taxation of King George.

One day back about 1957 somewhere in these United States, an unethical businessman walked into a hospital, took a look around and suddenly had a "light bulb over the head" moment. "Hey," he thought. "I believe I could make a pretty good profit out of this sick people thing," and health care was never the same. There exists no logical explanation for the cost of modern health care. NONE, regardless of any excuse made by corporate healthcare leaders . . . there exist absolutely no virtuous excuse. In all other industries, once technology enters the picture the costs associated with most products goes down . . . not with healthcare.

Traditionally, health care in America was affordable by anyone who needed it. The roots of modern health care in America actually began, like education, with many benevolent Christian organizations around the country. Churches all over the United States founded their own hospitals, homes for the elderly and invalids, medical institutions and even medical colleges in order to create local or community systems that would physically take care of ailing Americans like you and me. Many compassionate people who cared for others and their well being further established non-profit organizations and associations in the medical and psychological fields dedicated to the care of the sick and the insane with a goal to maintain health by eradicating illness and disease.

Some organizations such as "The Knights of the Order of Hospitaliers de John the Baptist" go as far back as the Crusades when a group of French monks established a place of refuge for sick and ailing Christians en route to the Holy Land in their attempt to expel invading Muslims from the city of Jerusalem. They later became an order of knights eventually known as the "Knights of Malta" or "Knights Hospitaliers" and their symbol, the Maltese-Cross, is today expressed by firefighters in the same aspect of caregivers and rescuers. We still see the remnants of the Church in the very names of many healthcare organizations such as Methodist, Presbyterian, Baptist, Catholic and Saints, yet there is no longer any hint of Christian compassion in any of these medical organizations once they turned into for-profit entities and became incorporated.

Unfortunately, the profit sector of big business moved in about the mid 20th century. The Church or benevolent non-profit organizations were rapidly replaced as more and more large and small privately owned hospitals and clinics began to be purchased by large for-profit medical organizations with a corporate mentality that shut down the small guys. Technology and the standard of care began to expand resulting in higher costs and bigger needs. Corporate boards and managed healthcare organizations began to emerge with a host of CEOs and administrators ready to take on the challenge of increased spending and stricter regulations with expensive operating costs which continue to rise annually. Hospitals began to close all across the nation unless they incorporated into large medical facilities. By the late 1980s, it was obvious that the only way a medical institution could survive was to join in with the secular big boys. This incorporation lead directly to higher profits for now-profit organizations and their investors which partly created a sky-rocketing healthcare cost adventure that has become completely out of control.

On the other end of the medical spectrum were the insurance companies who would offer very affordable health care plans that covered the whole family until two things happened simultaneously. One, health care costs began to rise and secondly, and most importantly, profits for the insurance companies and their investors and CEOs became more abundant as health care became a commodity. In the early days of health care, many people did not need insurance coverage as medical costs could be paid out in a few payments or in one low sum.

By the 1990s, insurance companies were no longer really insurance companies in the traditional sense. Some had become risk management companies who are now more interested in sustaining a level of profit than sustaining contractual agreements with their customers. Since that time, we have seen a battle between the opposing forces of corporate insurance companies vs. corporate medical organizations to see who can profit the most. In 2009, the top five U.S. health care firms boasted a 12.5 billion dollar profit, up 56 percent from 2008 whereas in the first three quarters of 2010, the top ten U.S. insurance organizations collectively boasted a 9.3 billion dollar profit. That was an increase of 41 percent since 2009. All the while, my premiums and deductable continue to rise and so do yours, that is, if you can afford medical insurance. Also, the advancement and dictatorial powers through risk management also saw the insurance companies creating a "third party" rule between patients and their doctors or pharmacists.

This process of unfathomable paperwork keeps our doctors and their staff tied up for more than 40 percent of the time just to please the insurance company in its attempt to keep from paying a claim or legitimately avoiding fraud and abuse. The result is more physician office staff, and that cost is passed on to the patient. Bottom line, if there were no profits to be made in insurance and health care, there would be neither, or at least it would not resemble anything like we see today.

In 1995 I had an appendectomy. I had health insurance through my employer, and the entire procedure cost me $52 out of pocket. In 2010, I had surgery on my shoulder. I still have insurance coverage through my employer, but my out of pocket expenses were near $3,000. And now the medical facility allows contractual doctors and other facilities to bill the patient individually so the average patient may receive eight to ten bills from health care professionals that they have never seen before. I even got a bill from a surgical nurse. What is up with that? Then I received a bill from a physician in another city that I had never heard of. After doing a little investigating, I discovered that while I was out like a light on the operating table, an attending physician came in to observe my surgery then had the gall to send me a bill for it. I politely explained to his office manager that such activity would be considered fraudulent and refused to pay the bill. The office manager told me they would extract the payment for services not rendered and apologized for the unfortunate mistake.

There is one fact that remains constant for all mankind, and that is that the human body is going to cease to function at some point. In others words, we are all going to die sooner or later. 100% of us will succumb to this reality. We all want that to be later as opposed to sooner. This desire is natural. However, under the current system of health care it is very costly.

In America, we spend approximately 2.5 trillion dollars annually on health care. That is 17.6 percent of our total economic output or GDP. That equates to approximately $8,160 a person each year just for coverage. If your employer covers your health care plan, he will spend over $14,000 a year on you and your family of four to have health care coverage, and that does not include your out of pocket expenses such as deductibles, prescription meds and various other procedures. The average family now pays as much for health care coverage annually as they pay on their mortgage. Over 2 million middle class families filed for bankruptcy in 2009. Of those, 52 percent were because of a major health crises in their family and of those, 75 percent had insurance. In most cases, people find out what their health care policy doesn't cover once they are denied the coverage after their premiums have been paid for some time. There is no one simple reason for high and rising health care costs. Health care in America is a commodity, and that may be where our biggest problem lies.

Malpractice lawsuits are a very integral part of health care costs today. The costs associated with malpractice are always passed on to the consumer in the sum of $75 billion annually which goes to pay for physician out-of-pocket costs, attorney litigation fees and payouts. Many physicians are performing "defense medical procedures" in order to avoid being sued by patients. This means delivering costly medical procedures and tests that are not necessarily needed for proper treatment. The result is a 3 percent increase in overall costs.

Another $150 billion is spent annually on obesity related illnesses. Obesity in America is one of the costliest aspects of health care today and is nothing more than a reflection of gluttony in our culture. The human body was not designed to carry 300 pounds of extra fat cells. The heart muscle has to work harder and harder to pump needed blood through all that extra tissue, subsequently wearing it out far before its time. As people become obese, they appear to look large on the outside, and they are, but their bone structure does not increase to compensate for the extra weight placing undue stress on joints, muscles, and tendons which results in all kinds of orthopedic diseases and maladies. The increased weight also shuts down the pancreas which is vital to breaking down sugars for glucose production increasing the advent of diabetes to the point of pandemic proportions. And this doesn't consider the amount of kidney and liver problems associated with obesity. A large portion of hospital and emergency room visits today can be directly or indirectly associated with obesity.

Another major modern health care problem is the abuse of the Medicaid and Medicare system. Fraud and abuse of these two vital systems has been reported to cost tax payers approximately $68 billion annually. Most of these costs are from overcharges by medical facilities, labs, clinics, hospitals and physician offices. Billing statements are traditionally full of mistaken overcharges added to patient charts by staff and physicians which basically go unnoticed and unchallenged by patients. Unfortunately, anytime the US government gets involved by creating well intended programs, fraud and abuse become rampant and the prices go through the roof.

Another $130 billion dollars goes to administer health care. This means building costs, maintenance costs, regulatory compliance, administrative fees, staff salaries, and salaries, perks and bonuses for upper management. One quarter to one third of your medical bill goes to pay for administrative costs and business practices. In total, malpractice costs, obesity, fraud and abuse of Medicaid and Medicare along with total administrative costs including executive pay scales are costing Americans approximately $423 billion each year. That is

20 percent of the total cost of health care. And if that isn't enough, more and more people simply are not paying their medical bills to the tune of over $70 billion a year. This is made up by higher premium costs to those who do pay via out-of-pocket medical deductible expenses which equaled approximately $250 billion in 2005 and is expected to nearly double by 2015.

One of the most astounding costs in healthcare is the consistent expanding costs of pharmaceuticals. This industry reaped over three billion dollars this year in psychotropic drug prescriptions alone. In the early days of psychiatry, the psychiatrist would counsel his patients or use other means of attempting to change the patients thinking in order to change their emotional patterns which were the underlying cause of most mental or emotional maladies. Today, with the advent of literally hundreds of new anti-psychotic or anti-anxiety drugs psychiatrists now take care of any mental or emotional challenge with drugs and these drugs can be lethal. In 2010, thousands of people died by suicide, homicide, or overdose while taking or coming off of psychotropic drugs.

In most cases, a person will walk into a psychiatrist's office where he will fill out a questionnaire which, in 20 minutes, will allow a psychiatrist the ability, in theory, to label that person with a serious mental diagnosis that he will carry for the rest of his or her life. Treatment of such diagnosis will be, naturally, with some kind of anti-anxiety or anti-depressive drug. The most common diagnosis being ADD, ADHD, Bipolar Personality Disorder, some common Anxiety Disorder, etc, all diagnosed from the manual called the DSM. This is all based on the theory of maladies caused by a so-called "chemical imbalance" in the brain of which there is absolutely no scientific instrument in which to measure. This is but an industry theory in which to label people and treat them with very powerful and mind numbing drugs that are in some cases killing people. There is absolutely no test in biology or chemistry and in no facets of the healthcare industry that proves that a chemical imbalance in the brain even exists for most people and is beginning to be challenged by many in the profession. But, for every new drug application processed through the FDA, there is now a hefty monetary application fee assessed to the drug company applying for approval. This is big bucks for the FDA. The drugs themselves, which actually cost pennies to manufacture, in most cases, will be sold by the pharmaceutical companies for four to five dollars a pill on average.

The key to the whole game is the doctor or psychiatrist who is marketed to by the drug companies to prescribe as many drugs to the general population as possible regardless of the terrible consequences perpetuated upon the unsuspecting public by this profiteering racket. The amount of prescription drugs in our culture today is the result of the best marketing campaign ever introduced by pharmacology upon the American people reaping billions in profits for those companies at the expense of addiction upon the masses.

But the big bite in healthcare which accounts for 75 percent of health care costs is chronic disease. 60 percent of those suffering from chronic disease are those people over the age of 65. Today, America has approximately 40 million seniors eligible for Medicare and Medicaid. By 2040, we will double that amount to approximately 80 million people. The cost to take care of this aging population will be staggering.

Health care is an essential need for people, as essential as police, fire and utilities. All of us will depend on some kind of health care at some point. Very few people can afford modern health care costs on their own when a crisis hits and they or someone they love becomes ill. We all need insurance, so we pool all our money together so when someone gets sick they can draw from the pool. That is what insurance is or was supposed to be. On average, private insurance companies take 15 to 22 percent of each premium dollar to pay for their administrative costs. And, just like the health care industry, administrative costs are used to pay salaries, the rent, purchase supplies, pay bills, postage, and pay out bonuses and dividends to investors and top-dog CEOs. A portion of those profits also go for political campaigns and lobbyists to fight insurance reform.

Most insurance companies are directly responsible to their investors because they are private, for-profit organizations, and they cannot make big profits by paying every claim that comes along or accepting people with existing conditions or life threatening problems that would be costly to maintain. So these companies can deny some claims and many procedures that do not make the small print or avoid foreseeable problem clients, all the while, protecting the bottom line which is, as you have discovered by now, corporate profits for investors, CEOs and other high level executives. These folks are paid well for their cleverness of creating very complicated and confusing formulas that ensure less payouts and more profit for the insurance companies. Once these corporations began to make massive amounts of money for those at the top, it had to be maintained with the consistent guarantee of growth over time. Now in order to guarantee those continued profits, your deductable and premium payments must increase annually to support the profit system. The guys at the top are not going to take a cut in pay. The insurance industry is not about your health. It is all about profit which is the bottom line. Insurance companies do not want health care costs to decline as it would cut into profit. Higher health care costs mean higher insurance premiums which equates to higher profits.

Insurance companies exist to make money, and they are making lots of it. And it does not matter if their insuring homes, health care or cars, the profits are there for the taking. But don't simply take my word for it. Just open your phone book and see for yourself how many insurance agents are listed in your community alone. And these are the low end of the insurance business. They are the guys and gals who are simply selling you the policy. The big money is on the corporate top of the insurance game. The bottom line is, insurance companies are not interested in lower costs for healthcare. It is the higher costs that result in corporate profits.

We have to respect President Obama for attempting to create a system to stop this problem, but the real problem, is not health care insurance coverage. Rather it is the "cost" of health care that is the problem and nobody seems to be addressing it. Once again, we have to understand that the cost of health care began to rise once corporate America muscled out the Christian Church and took over the healthcare industry transforming a once benevolent society into an insatiable profit hungry beast. You can purchase a bottle of Tylenol for $4.50, but if you are given merely two Tylenol tablets in the hospital the cost is marked up to $18.00, just for two over-the-counter mild pain relievers. INSANE! We once considered such an action theft or price gouging but if a corporation or a bank does it, it seems to be perfectly legal and socially acceptable.

Under the proposed health care plan, we will all be covered with no worries. Everyone will have health care. It is supposed that the government run, non-profit system of Medicare extracts only 2 to 3 percent from the tax dollar for administrative costs, and 0 percent for profit as opposed to what the private sector costs. That means more money goes for actually caring for the sick. The system, according to those proponents say the Medicare system is efficient and this is what our new government funded health care system will look like. Sounds good and noble? Think again! The Medicare system can barely manage to stay afloat and is bloated with bureaucratic red tape and corruption from one end to the other. Once again, the road to hell is paved with good intentions, and our government is classic for screwing up the simplest idea once it creates a government system from that idea. The only two things the government has ever been good at operating is the military and the IRS and that is it.

In a government run health care system, we will kiss quality and workmanship goodbye. With no competition and a highly regulated system, most health care workers will become typical government employees who find mostly disdain and contempt for the sick and will treat them so. We'll all be treated like we're in line for food stamps.

The problem with the government supported health care bill is, once again, it does not address the real problem of cost. The cost of health care and the future cost of guaranteeing a health care plan for every American based on the trending cost cannot be sustained. The plan will cost us billions of dollars of tax money by the year 2019, of which will be paid by each of us via higher taxes. Those who could suffer the most are the poor as they will be forced to purchase insurance or be fined by the US government through taxation. The insurance companies will be able to increase costs as they will monopolize upon the demands of the government. We should all have some kind of health care, but a government health care system that no one understands, even those who designed it, could have grave consequences.

> *"And I heard a voice from the fourth living creature saying, come and see, and I saw. A pale horse and the name that sat upon him was death and hell followed with him, and power was given to them over one fourth of the earth, to kill with sword, with hunger, with death and by the beasts of the earth."* Rev 6:7

Regardless of how we attempt to guarantee our health, one thing is for sure. Death will come to us all. Disease is rampant among the earth and always has been. As recent as the last century we saw a devastating pandemic sweep the globe taking millions of our population with it. In June 1917 the first case of the Spanish Flu was reported. By December 1920, it had resulted in the death of 50 to 100 million people worldwide and infected one quarter of the world's total population at the time. The disease created a "cytokine storm," or simply an over-reaction of the immune system which made those with the strongest immune systems most susceptible. Most of those who died were young, vibrant, healthy adults.

In the 1300's, the bubonic plague which began in China, was carried through the silk routes and by ships on the Mediterranean to Europe resulting in the deaths of over one third to one half of the European population. The "black plague" was characterized by huge black boils that covered the bodies of the infected who also presented with simple flu-like symptoms. The plague was caused by the bacterium "Yesinia pestis" and peaked in 1348.

In 2009, the first 31 cases of H1N1 virus was reported in North America. It had spread to 30 countries in two weeks. An additional 250,000 people die worldwide from the flu each year as 100,000 die from infections acquired in hospitals. 2 million people die each year from diseases which are preventable by simple vaccinations. Nearly one in five child deaths are contributed to dehydration brought on by diarrhea. Many of these people would have lived had they been able to obtain simple prescription antibiotics. My point: death is imminent and a daily occurrence.

But let's not be too hopeless. At some point, reality has a way of curving problems into solution finding adventures. Even if it means a total collapse of the health care industry, Americans will figure out some answers to the problem. But our first step must be to stop the profit system where health care is concerned or at least curb it to some degree, most likely through good ole competitive business practices which keep costs down. When the value of human health becomes nothing but a number on a corporate profit chart, we will cease to be human. I have no answers for health care costs other than to shop around to get the best deal, if you can find one. Unfortunately, for most Americans, the best deal is still unaffordable.

CHAPTER 15

THE WORKING MOTHER

NOW HERE IS A chapter that is going to ruffle some feathers, especially among those feminist who may have made the mistake of reading this. We hear it time and time again . . . "it takes both Mom and Dad working to make it now days" . . . and yes, that is true if you want to live deep in debt like the average American family. Does it really take two working to survive? Yes! If you think you need a new 2500 square foot home and two new cars in the driveway with a garage full of stuff, then it certainly does. But if you don't then perhaps there's another way to accept reality that doesn't include debt out the wazoo.

How much does a middle class working mother really financially help out the struggling family? Most women in the workplace without a degree and even some with a degree make approximately $22,000 to $32,000 annually working in dead end, meaningless service industry jobs in order to help pay those monthly bills, but is it really necessary? Does Mom working really help the family or does it create more problems, some of which will not be realized for years?

Women in the workplace are not the issue here. Many women have very productive careers that enhance the lives of their families in many ways, but many do not. Most middle class and poor women are not working for a career but because they have too. Many single mothers out there are forced to work and live on government assisted programs in order to survive. Many modern men have abandoned their responsibilities of head of household or fatherhood leaving their former wives and children to fend for themselves.

But, what about the married woman with children who has entered the workplace to better the family's financial situation? What is the real cost of her working? For the sake of argument let's just say we have a young working mother with two children who has gone back to work to help pay those bills. Dad has a steady job that brings home about $70,000 dollars a year. The house payment for the new three bedroom brick home is $1350 a month. Dad has a newer model truck with a monthly payment of $545, and Mom has to have transportation to get to work and back. Lord knows that in order to guarantee the safety and room for transporting two kids to all those activities requires some kind of late model SUV. So Mom's Tahoe with all the luxuries has a payment of $570 a month for six years.

Mom gets a job at a local bank as a teller. She is making a whopping $24,000 a year. But what is she really bringing home? The two little ones are four and seven years old. They have to go to daycare which runs the family $50 a week during the school year and $100 a week during the summer months. Then Mom has to have a decent wardrobe because the bank requires her to look presentable for customer relations. This will cost her an additional $3,000 annually to meet those fashionable expectations. Then there are the hair and nails that must be kept up which will add on another $1200 a year. There's also gas and maintenance expenses for Mom's car and by the time all the expenses are added, as we see below, Mom's financial contribution isn't what we thought it was.

$24,000 is Mom's annual salary at the bank
$2,880 this is what her taxes are going to be
$6,840 this is how much she will pay on her late model Tahoe SUV

155

$3,880 this is for fuel and maintenance for that SUV

$3,200 this is what she will spend on daycare

$3,000 this is what she will spend on wardrobe for work

$1,200 this is what she will spend on hair and nails for work

$1,456 this is what she will spend on dry cleaning

$960 this is what she will spend on eating at work (very conservatively)

Mom will actually spend $23,416 in order to have that job. She will actually add $584 to the family coffers this year. Mom is working for the sake of work or at least so she can have the "stuff" and something to do other than children. Most working mothers find themselves locked in a dead end service job because they are under the impression that it is something they must do.

This situation is extreme, I agree, but I chose it to make a point and to raise a question. Is it necessary for Mom and Dad both to work in most cases? In this particular case, no! It served this family not. The only thing it did was allowed a car finance company to make a lot of money at the whims of a family who is financially ignorant and pressured by society to behave so. Many mothers work because they are under the impression that their job is helping them obtain all the things that they desire in life when in actuality it is placing undue stress on the average family, placing families into debt and allowing daycares to raise our young. We have to ask ourselves, how necessary is it for Mom to enter the workplace, and if we are truly honest we will find it isn't as necessary as we have been taught.

Let me switch gears for a moment. In today's culture, the number one mental health disorder is by far Bipolar Personality Disorder, basically because it is one of the few mental disorders listed in the DSM (Diagnostic & Statistical Manual for Mental Disorders) that insurance companies will pay to treat on a consistent scale. Why are we seeing so many new cases of Bipolar Disorder these days? The answer to that is way beyond my expertise, but it doesn't take a water buffalo to see that perhaps it could be that there is a cash cow behind the symptoms of BPD which, closely parallel those of Reactive Attachment Disorder (a rarely heard of disorder in the world of pop psychology). The problem with Reactive Attachment Disorder is that it can only be confronted through relationship and serious specified child counseling, and no insurance company is going to dedicate resources for such treatment. Besides, no self-respecting pharmaceutical company would ever allow such a diagnosis that didn't call for some kind of chemical treatment to become a mainstream diagnosis.

According to Dr. Karen Purvis, Director of the Institute of Child Development at Texas Christian University, Reactive Attachment Disorder presents with many of the same symptoms as Bipolar Disorder. The problem is, not much is commonly known or accepted by general health care and insurance companies that would "popularize" Reactive Attachment Disorder (there is no money to be made from the treatment). It is suggested by some experts in child development that the disorder may originate, in some cases, in the womb and in a sense may be directly related to the mother–child relationship. I might be treading on thin ice here to suggest that working mothers could have some connection to behavior problems with children . . . after all, what a backwards philosophy, right? Maybe not!

Experts again suggested that there is a huge correlation between the time that a mother spends with her offspring and the proper development of those children. Just the gentle touch of a mother's love is a longing in every human being at birth and crucial to the continued development of a child. I am no child psychologist, but I don't have to be to see how important it is that a mother spend a lot of time . . . face to face, touching, engaging, teaching and loving those babies in the first few years of life.

The role of a mother in the home is crucial, and studies have shown that the absence of that mother's care for her children can and has been devastating. Mothers are extremely important to the family unit, and the absence of that consistent motherly love can be harmful. So, perhaps every family has to ask themselves, how important and needful is it to have Mom in the workplace? Many mothers do not have the choice, but some do and those are the ones that can make a difference.

The toughest job in the world is that of a stay-at-home Mom. It requires unlimited hours of exhausting work much of which will seem to go unappreciated. Washing clothes, ironing, changing diapers, cooking, grocery shopping, day in and day out can seem monotonous and completely unglamorous and it is. Like I said, it is the toughest job in the world and certainly not for many women, especially in our self indulged climate that tells women that they can be worldly successful and raise a family too. That may be a lie. You have to choose one or the other but you cannot have both. Your nanny and house maid may help you look like you have achieved both but you haven't. It's one or the other. We can all make babies but a true heart-felt relationship can only be found by presence. You have to be there, not the daycare, not the nanny, not the teacher, not the housekeeper and especially, not your mother and father. We can certainly make cases for individuals, here and there, who may seem to have accomplished both and tend to have very emotionally healthy families, but this is not the norm but rather an exception to a culture with serious moral and ethical problems. It may sound judgmental and speculative but these are the hard cold facts.

Many families do not count the cost of Mom in the workplace. It can be more expensive, emotionally and spiritually as well as financially for Mom to have to go to work in a two parent family. This is a call each family has to make for themselves but I challenge you to put the numbers to paper and see if it's worth the stress and the loss of mom at home.

You may consider downsizing the cars and the house. None of your neighbors care about what you drive or how big your house is.

They only care about what they drive and how big their house is. Once you begin to realize that most two parent working families are sacrificing the emotional health of their children for the sake of stuff, you can begin to get things prioritized. Children want Mom and Dad, not stuff, unless that is all they know, then stuff replaces Mom and Dad and will replace relationships for the rest of their lives. They will never have enough stuff and may struggle with the emptiness of one ruined relationship after another, as they will be susceptible to addictions and streams of crisis all of their own making.

CHAPTER 16

WHAT NOW?

By now you are most likely wondering what you can do to begin your ascent up the debt free ladder of life. How do you become DEBT FREE? The first thing is to understand the two ancient secrets of the rich. I am going to share this mystical doctrine that has only been known by the wealthy since the dawn of man. These two key elements to wealth have been closely guarded by those who know how to obtain vast amounts of it, but I am willing to expose this secret of eons to the masses. Are you ready? First, stop spending money! And secondly, know that there are NO secrets of the rich and there never have been, especially in the United States. There you have it, now go forth and prosper.

That's right! There are absolutely no secrets of the rich. We have all seen books written and seminars given on the secrets of the rich. The only people who get rich via this process are the people writing the books and giving the seminars to suckers looking for some easy way to wealth. There simply aren't any. You can't make money working just two to three hours a day and you're not going to become rich using other people's money. You can't spend your way into prosperity and if anyone is telling you that, he is a liar and most likely selling you something. Any time someone is trying to convince you to invest in something, always question his motive. Most likely, there is profit involved for him. This includes doctors, attorneys, real estate agents, televangelists, your broke brother-in-law and any other snake willing to embellish or exaggerate the truth for profit.

The world is a harsh and troubled place with constant traps and snares. It isn't so much what you know that can be dangerous but what you don't know that will be used against you. People are in debt not because they don't know how to purchase stuff; rather they do not understand the financial implications surrounding a life of consumerism. Let's say you are going to take a trip through the deepest jungles of the Congo. Sounds exciting, so you show up for the trip carrying several bags and wearing your new cargo shorts and latest hiking boots. After all, that's how they did it in the old Tarzan movies. The natives look at you and smirk and hope you have prepaid for their services because they know you aren't going to last two hours on this trip.

You are uninformed and ill equipped for the mission. One who knows the jungle understands that it is unwise to wear shorts in such thick foliage. The sharp ends of plants will tear into your exposed flesh and the mosquitoes are going to have a heyday, as are the leeches. You have no bug repellant and no clue of life on the forest floor which is teaming with hundreds of thousands of man-eating insects just waiting on a sucker like you. That is how life works, no matter where we are. You must be ready for the obstacles that are going to be in the way on your journey. Whether its mountain climbing, sailing, politicking, or even marriage, you'd better be prepared for what you are in for or the realities of life will devour you. The world of finance works exactly by the same rules as the jungle, and you must be constantly aware of the dangers with the ability to identify the predators and where they lurk so you can avoid them.

The financial jungle has many predators with the banks being the most dangerous of them all. We have often read that the "Lion is the King of the Jungle," which is silly because lions don't live in jungles. Their natural habitat is on the plains . . . but regardless, the banks are the kings of their jungle and you must be equipped to deal with their hunting techniques or you will become their dinner. The game for financial survival exists. It is real and everybody plays . . . everybody! You will either be a winner or a loser, but you will play never-the-less. If you do not understand the game and its rules, you will be devoured. I have given many examples in this work to help prepare you for your journey or at least give you a roadmap to a safer route. Yes, safer routes do exist but you must be informed as there are no road signs and no G.P.S. in this jungle.

The most important thing you must do is educate yourself in personal finances. It is said that rich men own big libraries while poor men own big screen televisions. This is very true and reflective of our belief systems covered in a previous chapter. For many years I was a front line firefighter. One day my crew and I responded to an emergency medical situation at a small, dilapidated house. While we were treating the patient I couldn't help but notice the size of the television in the tiny living room. It was huge! I took note in an attempt to figure out how they got it into that room. That is still a mystery, but the fact is so many people have completely messed up priorities.

The first thing you must do is educate yourself in every facet of financial literacy where your personal finances are concerned and get your priorities in order. If you live in a 500 square foot shack and have a television the size of an entire wall, then you may have some priority issues. On the same level, if you are living in a new 2300 square foot house with two late model vehicles in the driveway and a garage full of stuff all the while living in perpetual debt to have it all, then you might have priority issues. The middle class in America is suffering from serious priority issues. It is the middle class that is causing its own collapse by its own debt, not the poor!

You must learn how to say NO to yourself. The next time you are at the mall and see that "darling pair of shoes," ask yourself how bad you really need them. This is something I learned that worked very well for me once I decided to get myself out of debt. Every time I considered making a purchase I would automatically ask myself how badly I needed it. That was one of my first steps to financial freedom. I found myself putting many items back on the shelf then found myself avoiding stores all together unless I absolutely needed an item.

You must then understand that you do not need more than one credit card. This is imperative, and it is also a must that both husband and wife be on the same page financially or you will forever argue over finances. Many divorces have occurred over financial problems in marriage. If you are not absolutely honest with your spouse about money, they are going to feel taken advantage of and this is going to set the stage for a long drawn out fight which will never be resolved.

Never carry a credit card that your spouse does not know about . . . ever! Credit cards are dangerous and should have warning labels on them just like cigarettes. Store cards are very expensive and must go. You DO NOT NEED THEM. They charge far more in interest than a single bank card such as Visa or MasterCard. Sit down, lay all your credit cards out on a table, take a pair of scissors and cut them up. This is a knife into the jugular vein of the bank, and your first blow in the fight for survival. Keep one credit card, or at least one for each spouse if you must and do not use them unless you need them. You must learn to become disciplined if you ever plan to get out of debt, and that discipline begins with the credit card. DESTROY them all because they are destroying you. Once again, you only need one and make absolutely sure, without a doubt that you pay it off in full each and every month and only use it for must purchases. Pay everything else in cash. Remember, you can't overextend cash and the overextending is what got you into this mess.

Once again, and this is absolutely crucial, if you are married, you must be willing to be one hundred percent honest with your spouse about money. Hiding information is deceitful and a sign of immaturity and fear and will most definitely cause marital problems. You must grow up in your relationship and step up to the plate and do your part. Keeping one credit card hidden from your spouse will have untold consequences.

Trust is most important. You must be absolutely honest with each other about the credit cards and spending. You must both be on the same page. And both are going to have to give up the luxuries of life if you really plan to get out of debt. This may mean no new clothes for a while, no new shoes, hair dos, nails, no hunting trips, no ski trips, no cruises, no eating out, no golf, no movies, no clothes taken to the cleaners, etc. You must tighten up all spending if you are going to become debt free. Once you are debt free and figure out how to stay that way, then you deserve the luxuries of life, but be absolutely honest and work as a team or your adventure will never begin. But "Hey, who's going to iron the clothes if we can't take them to the cleaners?" You are! It means you're going to have to develop another life skill and buy a can of spray starch and break out the ole ironing board. This will require getting up off the couch. You may even want to get rid of cable TV for a while which may require reading a book. Several people I know have rid themselves of cable TV and told me how their life at home changed dramatically. They began to talk to each other, spend time with each other, help their children with homework and found time to read and educate themselves on different subject matter. They began to live.

The biggest mistake people make with credit cards is carrying a large balance on the card each month and paying it off at the end of that month, never understanding that the bank is counting on an emergency in your life that will disable you the ability to make the full payment and then they will have you. Pay your bills by check and mail them in as this will lower the risks of identity theft. Pay with cash for things like groceries, clothes and everyday needs. Never, ever, ever, use credit cards for fast food. Every time you use your card, the card company gets a fee from the place you are making the purchase from further extending profits for them. Every time the card is swiped . . . cha-ching! You must understand how to alleviate the credit card's power over your life.

Something else Americans do not understand is that the garage was designed as a place to put the car. Most garages are so full of stuff that there is no room for a vehicle. This means garage sale! Think of it this way: most of what you own takes up space and goes unused. If you haven't used it in the last year and a half, then you most likely do not need it. A good garage sale can alleviate that issue and net a family just the right amount of money to start paying off their smallest debt. This is what Dave Ramsey calls the debt snowball. It is a very simple way to start your climb out of debt. Take all your monthly debt and write it down. Categorize the debt from the most expensive, usually the house, down to the least, most likely a credit card or other revolving debt. Then, pay off the least expensive first, making minimum payments on all the others. Once the smallest debt is paid for, it does not mean that you now have extra cash to spend on stuff. It means you are going to roll that savings into the next higher debt until you pay it off, then take that savings and roll it into the next higher debt and pay that off until the point that you get to the house and once you have paid it off . . . you are a free person.

This may seem an impossible feat but let me assure you it can and is being done by thousands of Americans who are tired of living in bondage to debt. It is essentially difficult and takes intense focus, but everyone who wants to be debt free will be using this method. It can be done, I am living proof. Remember, "LIFE IS HARD." The amazing thing is, like most blessings, it did not take half the time I thought it would take. Once you become focused and really start seeing the benefits of the plan working in your favor, it begins to magically pick up steam like a locomotive. Once it gets going, it's hard to stop unless you do something stupid.

It is imperative to set up a budget and stick with it. This means no fancy vacations regardless of how much you think you need to get away. Don't . . . not until you are debt free. Then you can take a vacation to any place and pay for it all with cash, just like the wealthy, and why? Because you will be wealthy! Remember, wealth is measured not so much by one's holdings, rather by how much he is leveraged. Those with no debt are considered wealthy, not those with a lot of toys. If you are working to become debt free, you are working your way to wealth. Your children will not have long term psychological damage if they do not get to see Disney World on a credit card. The best gift you can give your children is your love and your time which cannot be a commodity. Teaching them to live debt free and out of bondage to the banks is paramount to their future.

Many times I have seen families max out those credit cards every Christmas to purchase stuff for friends and relatives and then take half a year to pay off the bill. This is foolishness. Next year explain to the extended family that there will be no gift exchange from your side until you can become debt free. If they love you they will understand and just may follow your lead. If not, too bad. A family budget will be a must, and you must stick with it no matter what. Do not plan on spending money unless you have an emergency . . . Christmas and birthdays are NOT emergencies. Your teenage daughter going on a trip with her BFF is NOT an emergency. Your son getting the hottest video game just on the market is NOT an emergency. Remember "PRIORITIES." Once you are debt free, you can give and you can buy those gifts with cash, the righteous way.

One extremely important thing to becoming debt free is establishing a savings account. Why? Because as we have already seen, life is going to happen! Within three months time something is going to happen that will require that savings, especially if you have children. Many experts suggest six months of your current salary in an emergency account . . . yea right, if you're JP Morgan. This is not possible for struggling families deep in debt. I suggest that you do the best you can to create an emergency account of at least $1,000. How? By doing what you have to do . . . remember "LIFE IS HARD," ignoring that fact got you into debt to begin with. So you need to sell something, i.e., garage sale, the boat, the watercraft, the four-wheeler, the hunting lease, the cat . . . no one will buy a cat so it may have to be the dog, whatever. If you don't have anything to sell then you may have to get a second job, temporarily, just to create an emergency account to cover insurance deductibles or any other unforeseen misfortune. It can be done, but you are going to have to get creative which will require getting up and doing something about your particular situation. This will require massive amounts of self- responsibility and action on your part, as well as hard work and radical dedication. So, if you are reading this book for entertainment I recommend putting it down now.

Downsizing is another must-be project for the soon-to-be debt free family, part of which can be accomplished by the garage sale as mentioned earlier, but another idea could be getting out from under a costly car payment. We saw in the chapter on the car payment how much financial waste is exemplified by the average family through the over-priced automobile. Small and medium-sized vehicles are just as easy to get around in as a gas-guzzling SUV. Besides, every time some Arab prince has heartburn, gas prices rise and with growing uncertainty in the Middle East, they may not come down. Gas prices from four to five dollars a gallon (or more) could be in our future. That is going to have a serious impact on big gas hogs.

Many folks are upside down in their notes for expensive cars until well into the payment plan but once able to get rid of that big car note consider purchasing a smaller and more economically-feasible-used-car. $600 dollar a month payments for six years while paying interest to a bank is not in your best interest and is stealing your wealth and your family's future. Suffer for a while and get rid of the money hog. Remember, keeping up with the Jones's is always going to be a losing proposition for you. You do not need heated seats. You aren't going to die if your butt gets cold while waiting on the heater to warm up.

Americans survived for years with cars that didn't have the luxury of a double-cheek-heater.

Another huge mistake people make is purchasing seasonal recreation vehicles like boats, watercrafts, four wheelers and motorcycles. These items are no problem if you don't owe money on them, however, if you have a vehicle that you can only use three months out of the year but have to make monthly payments twelve months out of the year, then that is a problem. This is simply throwing your money away. The wealthy do not think that way with their money. Remember, if you are making payments, you are making the banks money on interest for something that just sits in your garage or back yard most of the time.

You may even want to consider downsizing your home. If you are living in a new upscale subdivision because it's a swanky spot, then reconsider how much you are costing your family and your children. There are many other cheaper neighborhoods with much cheaper taxes. Many think that they live where they do because of good schools, but in most cases that simply isn't true, especially in small towns where every school is part of the Independent School District and one school is no different than the other. You must consider the size of the home, the mortgage spent over 30 years and the taxes paid annually, and make your decision. It may be much cheaper to live in a less expensive area. The savings, for those who really want to become debt free could be extreme, resulting in money back into your account instead of the banks. Over years, this could change the condition of your family tree setting your children up with a much brighter and more secure future. The cost of living in an exclusive neighborhood could cost you your child's college tuition in a matter of 20 years in just property taxes alone.

Another smart move is auto and home insurance savings. You can easily save $400 to $1200 annually just by shopping around for insurance. All you have to do is go online and Google "insurance quotes." The next thing you will have is dozens of insurance companies sending you quotes that are going to most likely knock your socks off. For years I went with the same insurance company because they gave me a discount by placing our home and cars on the same carrier, and I was under the impression that my loyalty meant something to that company . . . Wrong! Insurance companies could care less about loyalty, regardless of their commercials. They are big business making big money, and you don't mean squat to them.

I found numerous other companies that would do the same for a third of the cost. Bye-bye old company and hello to the new who saved me over $600 annually on my home and auto insurance. That much money would go a long way to a person who is serious about getting out of debt by allocating those funds toward becoming debt free. Another good tip is to look closely at your policy and make sure you're not double paying for things. Many people are over-insured and do not realize it. For instance, most mortgage companies require PMI (Private Mortgage Insurance) upon the initiation of the loan but never explain that once 20 percent of the loan is paid the PMI is no longer required. The insurance companies do not advertise this fact. Check to make sure you aren't paying for unnecessary insurance premiums. Get the highest deductible possible but make sure you have that amount in a savings plan in the event you have to cover it. Raising your deductibles can save you quite a bit of money each year.

Smart people constantly look for ways to save money. Many families use coupons when buying groceries, and I highly recommend taking the time to do so. But be careful with coupons as many can induce the buyer to purchase things they don't need just because they have a coupon. A smart shopper will easily tell the difference and understand that the right coupons can save you literally hundreds of dollars a year. Another tip is stop buying frozen or prepared food at the supermarket. These items are costly for the sake of convenience. Take the time to cook food at home. An inconvenience I know but remember "Life is Hard." This will take time and effort but another reason to get off the couch and turn off that television and it's a great opportunity to involve the whole family in the process making for great family time every night.

Another good tip is to give up the ATM. If you need cash, get to the bank during working hours and write a check for cash because you are charged a fee at most banks to use your own money via the ATM. You would be surprised how much you spend annually just getting your money out of your account using the ATM. Then understand that many families spend a lot of money on expensive household cleaning items that smell good. The basis of all cleaning items sold in the store is usually bleach or ammonia. Go on-line and Google home cleaning supplies and you will be amazed of what you can make with simple household bleach to clean with. WARNING: never mix bleach and ammonia together when cleaning, they do not like each other.

Stop buying new clothes every time the seasons change. Nobody really cares what you wear as long as it doesn't have holes in it or it doesn't smell bad. People who worry about what others wear are out of touch with reality and usually very superficial. Truly wealthy people have no respect for the fashion conscious and in most cases consider them egotistical people that can't do math. Clothes have become very expensive, and some Americans now have closets the size of shacks in third world countries that sleep a family of six. There is something wrong with that. If you will notice, most garage sales are dumping clothes more than any other item because we are saturated with clothes.

Most of us do not wear half of what we own, perhaps another place to downsize. And buying name brand clothes when you have to do it on a credit card is completely financially foolish. There are many stores today that sell consignment clothing such as Salvation Army. Nobody cares where you buy your clothes and if they do, they aren't the kind of people you should want to be friends with. People who put stock in such thinking are simply immature, egotistical and selfish and most likely broke and deep in debt to credit cards.

Know this, spending is habitual and has become an addiction to most Americans. We have been programmed over our lifetimes to spend and we are habitually addicted to it. Like any addiction, it takes a lot of painful work to change our thinking. The battle here is for our minds, and it is a brutal fight. You must change your money habits if you are ever going to rid yourself of the bank and its bondage on your family. You must be prepared to think differently, to create a new inner person that is independent and strong. You must be willing to see the lies that placed you into bondage and identify the predators through some kind of re-education process. Your perspective of wealth and what it is must change, and you must become disciplined enough to endure the pain of battle in order to stand up to the evil that is your enemy. The fight for freedom is grueling, but those who begin to get a taste of that freedom know no other recourse than to consistently pursue it.

Pain and discomfort are exactly what you will experience once you make the conscience decision to become debt free. But, this is only a short withdrawal experience. Stick with it and a new way of life will emerge for you and your family. Prosperity and wealth are there for you simply by your choice and it does not matter how poor you think you are. Every person in America deserves to be free from debt and that includes YOU regardless of your situation. You can obtain financial freedom. Once you are free, you will find you have power over things you never thought possible. You will discover that you do not need the US government as much as you did when in debt. Just like our forefathers, you will experience a sense of freedom you never thought possible. Stress will be reduced tenfold, and there will be no more arguing over finances and the silly things that destroy the marriage where money is concerned. It is a difficult road and only the determined will make it. You have to ask yourself, are you one of the determined?

Avoid consolidated loans. Many bankers urged folks to take out consolidated loans in order to wrap all the bills into one monthly payment that usually resulted in a lower sum of all totaled. The reason this usually doesn't work is because those borrowing the money haven't changed their spending habits and tend to go right back into the same spending pattern adding more revolving debt right on top of that consolidated loan perpetuating their problem.

Lastly, do not, and I mean, DO NOT fall for the scammers who claim that they can clean up your credit score or take care of your debt for a fee. This makes as much sense as paying an attorney so you can declare bankruptcy. Nobody can clean up your credit. NOBODY! If you have bad credit it is because, for whatever reason, you did not pay your bills. Most non-payment hits or slow-pay hits are going to stay on your credit history for four to seven years in most states. Sort of like breaking a mirror; you're going to have seven years of bad financial luck. There is nothing anyone else is going to do to help your debt problem that you can't do yourself.

Many companies claim they can clean up your debt problem. YOU can clean up your debt problem alone without their costly assistance. These people do not have a special formula, nor do they play golf with your creditors. You are going to have to make the time and the phone calls but understand, most creditors simply want you to pay what you owe. Contact them and work out some kind of pay plan. Such action is taking responsibility for your situation, and it shows credibility on your part. Your ability to communicate with them can make all the difference in the world. That is just the way it is.

Here are a few tips to help you save money and start your debt free journey:

- Cut up those credit cards, you only need one
- Begin your snowball plan
- Create and stick to a budget
- Sell on eBay, some people are making this a new profession
- Do not borrow for things that lose value
- Stop eating out and take your lunch to work
- Consider downsizing your house
- Get rid of gas guzzling high payment vehicles

- Start an emergency savings account
- Use cash instead of a credit card
- Never do business with rent-to-own establishments
- Never do business with quick cash establishments
- Cancel magazine subscriptions
- Understand the difference between wants and needs
- Live below your means
- If you can't pay cash, do not buy it
- Ask yourself, how bad do I really need it?
- Shop around for insurance quotes on home and auto
- Get a second job to create your emergency account
- Do not purchase luxuries that steal from you and your family
- Have a garage sale
- Teach your children to save
- Plant a garden
- Change filters on the home A/C every six weeks
- Turn all electrical items off in your home when you are not using them
- Invest in surge protectors for all your electrical items
- Bundle the cable, phone and internet services
- Get a slower internet speed
- Consider getting rid of your home phone
- Use coupons when shopping
- Use eBates for up to 25 percent off on shopping
- Get your books at the library
- Replace incandescent light bulbs with Compact Fluorescent Bulbs (WARNING: do not purchase bulbs made in China, they are a fire hazard, make sure they are UL listed)
- Switch your banking account from a large bank to a smaller local bank
- Always shop with a list and stick to it
- Never shop when you are hungry, ever!
- Drink more water (do not buy bottled water for your home)

- Always buy generic when possible
- If you have to eat out, get take home and don't purchase drinks
- Don't purchase expensive cleaning products
- Wash the vehicles at home and avoid expensive carwashes
- Set the lawn mower on the highest setting, this allows the grass to hold more moisture
- Don't keep large dogs that are expensive to house and feed
- Only purchase Christmas gifts for immediate family
- Keep a constant eye on your spending
- Know where your money is going
- Move your account from a bank to a credit union if possible
- Know the Banker is NOT YOUR FRIEND
- Do not purchase brand new cars
- Don't borrow money . . . ever! (I know you think this one is not possible, but try it)

These are just a few things you can do to save money or stop spending all together so you can get out of debt. Google websites for ways to save money and make an investment in one of Dave Ramsey's books on personal finances, you'll find his advice the best in the business and he has helped thousands of Americans change their way of looking at finances and given them a clear pathway out of debt. Once you are debt free and learn to stay that way, then you can purchase whatever you wish and pay cash for it and nothing in the world beats paying for something with cash.

Lastly, a very important but painful process is to determine your financial worth. This may be disappointing at first but can work as a motivator to begin your debt riddance program. Take a sheet of paper and list all your debts on one side. On the other side list all your assets, things that have monetary value that you own outright. Add the two columns up and subtract the debts from the assets. This is your net worth. Do not be surprised if you find yourself in the negative. You are exactly where most Americans are. This is the crux of the problem in our country today as the average American home is leveraged way beyond its means.

The goal is to increase the asset column and decrease the debt column. In time you will move to the positive side of the list as long as you stay focused on becoming debt free and ridding yourself of credit cards, student loans, car payments, etc. Once you become seriously focused on becoming debt free and begin the process, it should take approximately seven years on paper to complete. But that's on paper. In reality most people do it in half that time once they see how it is changing their lives.

Below is a "net worth" example of a newly married, college educated, upwardly mobile American couple with professional jobs living in a new upper-middle-class neighborhood. This young couple is dripping with opportunity but ignorant of the financial predators. This, unfortunately, is the American way. Their assets, which are few, are listed in the column on the left while their debts, which are many, are listed on the right.

Average American Net Worth

Assets		Debts	
Car	$6,000	Credit Card	$6,300
Jewelry	$3,800	Credit Card	$4,380
Savings	$1,500	Credit Card	$1,200
Retirement	$20,000	Student Loan	$28,000
		Student Loan	$36,000
		Car	$32,000
		Car	$18,000
		Mortgage	$128,000
		Boat	$11,000
		Equity Line	$18,000
Total	**$31,300**		**$282,880**

So the net worth of this couple, though they appear to be on the upper end of things, is actually minus $257,780. That's $257,780 in debt (in the red). So the next time you drive by that young couple's home in a new upper class addition and wonder how all those people afford to live that way, just remember what the average debt for the average family really looks like. Many young or newly married Americans are living way beyond their means and, are deep in debt to have what it took their parents 40 years to acquire and thanks to the banks, they can look as if they have it all under control.

As you can clearly see, this is not a good place to be but this is the current situation for most college educated families today. And these two don't have children yet. They are considered young urban professionals who both attended good four-year universities and have professions that result in a combined salary of approximately $145,000 a year which is around $90,000 above the national average. This couple making that kind of money should be enjoying life to the fullest because they should be free and easy to do so. But alas! They are the typical American family who believe they must have nice things and go to exotic places on vacation each year, and our current financial climate allows just that.

They also believe they should drive a late model SUV and a BMW as an example of their cultural status. They are under the impression that they deserve to live in a very nice upscale neighborhood in a suburb made just for folks like them. After making the house payment, the vehicle payments and the student loans there just isn't much left at the end of the month for spending money, so credit cards have saved the day for this outwardly and upwardly mobile couple. As you can see, the revolving debt and the ski boat along with the loan made against the equity in the home (which made a down payment on the ski boat) has left this upwardly mobile couple stuck in a prison of debt. And the banks were more than happy to put them there. After all they're young, they make good money, they have college degrees and they are a good investment for the banker who knows he'll have these two suckers for life.

This couple isn't necessarily greedy or careless, yet they are programmed to do exactly as they have done by our current system of perpetual debt. Like all of us, they have been taught by the financial institutions and the corporate culture to live beyond their means. Since they were small, they were instructed and indoctrinated to follow the banking trail right down the financial rabbit hole of debt. College boards, credit card companies, auto financers, and corporate banks along with constant advertising have instructed this unfortunate pair to their financial slaughter and like unsuspecting moths to the flame, they did just as their nature lead them to do.

The marriage counselor was not added to the list here, but may be a viable player in the game as the stress from debt will be a huge burden on their marriage. Most couples fight over financial problems more than any other issue in the home today.

The example above is, unfortunately, reflective of the average American household, and this one doesn't even have the expenses that come with children. So don't feel bad when you sit down and add up your assets vs. debts. Once you have done that you can see where you need to improve and get to work on a budget and debt snowball plan, and BE PREPAIRED TO LIVE WITHIN YOUR MEANS. Remember, the whole process may take up to seven years but for most that get radical with it, it takes half that time. Start with the small stuff and pay it all off, regardless of interest until you get to the cars then at last, the house. Then you will be among the truly wealthy, and your life will definitely change as will the lives of your children.

America is the land of opportunity. You have the opportunity to become debt free if you are willing to do what it takes. You will have to make it happen as there are no gimmies in debt free. You will have to work for it. Roll up your sleeves, get radical, make a plan and stick with it. In order to get to where you want to go you must first know where you are and how to get to where you want to be. You begin with understanding your net worth. Debt free is where you want to be, and your net worth is the beginning of the journey. Knowing where you are going and how to get there is extremely important and must be part of your plan. Understanding the dangers and predators along the path is also very important but will be part of that journey. Educate yourself well and avoid the dangers in order to safely reach that debt free destination.

Be aware of anyone who gives you any kind of financial advice that entails any kind of spending or revolving debt. Understand their motive and in almost 100% of the time, that person is himself deep in debt or not far behind. As Dave Ramsey says, "Never take financial advice from your broke brother-in-law." The only way to becoming debt free is to stop spending money.

CHAPTER 17

GIVING

"For true love is inexhaustible; the more you give, the more you have. And if you go to draw at the true fountainhead, the more water you draw, the more abundant is its flow." **Antoine De Saint-Exupery**

GIVING IS THE MEANS of gaining. It is the responsibility of all mankind to give, especially the wealthy and once you become part of the wealthy (those who live debt free, not necessarily those who are rich), you too will be able to give. Many times growing up I was compelled to give to those who I believed had nothing, but I couldn't because I was, unbeknownst to me, one of them. Then, once I became a middle-class working adult I was still compelled to give to those less fortunate than myself but couldn't because I was still one of them, but this time it wasn't because I lacked materialism. Rather I was so in debt and strapped to monthly payments that I lacked the ability to give. Once I paid my bills each month, I had nothing left for the needy and began to believe the false idea (as many Americans have today) that I was the needy.

You can't help others if you are strapped to monthly debt. That's one reason, other than idolatry, that debt is a sin because it keeps us from doing God's will which is to give of ourselves. Americans are known for giving, especially rich Americans who have established thousands of not-for-profit foundations for the betterment of mankind because they were entrusted with spirits of philanthropy. Great libraries, schools, hospitals, endowments and trusts set up for the humanities has assisted our thriving culture, and even today we see millions and millions of dollars given by the top 10 percent of Americans going toward humanitarian efforts.

But Christ had a different idea of giving. He told the parable of the "Widow's Mite", giving us insight to giving God's way. The story is told of a rich man who gave much but sacrificed hardly anything whereas a lone and poor widow cast two mites (the smallest of coin) which was all she had, she gave out of poverty. The story is not about how much we give, yet why we give and the sacrifice we commit while giving. The rich man gave much but sacrificed nothing. The widow gave all and sacrificed everything yet trusted God to meet her needs. The wealthy man gave materially but the widow gave through faith. Earthly giving may help earthly things but giving from the heart is giving God's way. Perhaps it isn't about how much one gives rather how much one has left after giving.

When I was a child times were financially tough on our family and it was not uncommon to have little food in the house or funds to pay the electric bill as several times our electricity was cut off for lack of payment. At one time we lived directly across the street from a large church. My father was not in the picture and my mother was struggling just to keep food on the table. Those good folks never once knocked on our door. Not that they had any obligation to do so, but churches and other organizations all over America send monies and assistance to foreign countries, which is a good thing, yet they rarely consider the needs of those who live right across the street, right in their own neighborhoods. I once read about a preacher who would go door to door all over his city inviting people to his church until he realized that he had never knocked on the house next door to his own. There were people on his own street that he didn't even know and they too had many needs. Pain and suffering may be much closer than you think. There are needs throughout the world but perhaps our best efforts to meet those needs should start right in our own neighborhoods and communities.

Drug abuse, poverty, teen pregnancy, crime, hunger, ignorance, disease, isolation, loneliness and many other problems are never going to be solved on the state or national level. The government or some lofty organization is never going to rid the world of these things no matter how much money we throw at the situation. These are your problems. These are the problems of your neighborhood, your community and your city . . . not the federal government. The kid across the street with a bad attitude is as much your problem as he is the police departments. We must get involved if we are ever going to eradicate problems in our own communities. This is how America did it for years. They got involved, forged relationships and created problem solving groups and affiliations. They got the job done in their own neighborhoods and communities. In many cities and states, the Christian Church lead the way.

It is easy to give to this organization or that organization because it usually takes little to no sacrifice on our part. We write a check, throw in a twenty here and there and go on with our lives believing that we have done our part in helping out. But God doesn't necessarily need your money. He needs YOU! He expects you personally to get involved, to roll up your sleeves and get your hands dirty. He expects you to take the risks and be a participant, not necessarily your money or a lofty organization. He expects each of us to be a "good Samaritan."

But I will be the first to admit we have a new problem in this country of plenty. Identifying those truly in need. Who are the needy? Who are the people who really need our help? Many believe they are needy when they are not, at least not physically. There are very few skinny or mal-nourished people waiting in the soup line in this country where obesity has become a major issue. In the time when Christ walked the earth, the culture was an extension of Rome and Romans were a tiny step up from barbaric. If a woman lost her husband, she could easily starve. If a child lost his parents, there were no foster homes or orphanages save work houses where some of the children would be horribly abused or sold into slavery. If one was unfortunate enough to be born with some kind of disability and had no family or support system, his only hope would be to beg the general public for his basic needs or starve to death. And if one became ill and his family could not afford a doctor, he simply died. Jesus came at a time when people knew nothing of human rights, and the religious leaders could label anyone an outcast simply on the basis of disease or reputation or by a sin his father committed.

Today we have social systems in America designed to help the poor and less fortunate, and those systems are overtaxed and terribly abused. Most social challenges where historically handled on a community level but are now charged to state or federal governments. Medicare, Medicaid, Social Security, and other social programs are draining us through taxation and those programs continue to grow. It has become very easy for us to sit back and allow the government to take care of more and more Americans while we complain about taxation. God never intended for the government to take care of us. My question here again is, who are the needy? Just last week I was talking to a homeless man when we were interrupted by his cell phone. It was a friend of his who was also homeless calling on his cell phone! Some people making six figure incomes consider themselves needy because they have terribly mismanaged their finances and believe they are lagging behind because their high-end lifestyle is at risk. Perhaps these are the poor in spirit Christ spoke of on the "Sermon on the Mount" and they may be the neediest of all but certainly not of monetary or worldly gifts.

Then there are many who learn how to use the system through fraudulent means all the while stealing from those truly in need. But what about those CEO's leading so-called charitable organizations while reaping many of the dollars donated for a cause and justifying it for executive pay and expenses? The very idea is socially acceptable in today's business culture but what if Jesus would have had that same mindset? Can you imagine Christ negotiating his annual salary with his overpaid attorney sitting next to him at the table demanding his rationalized reward for all that healing and salvation? Oh, he sort of did have a guy on his staff who thought that way, his name was Judas.

Each year regular folks just like you and me are urged to donate to local, state and national charities such as The United Way, The American Heart Association or The Endowment for the Humanities. And Americans are quite generous to the tune of billions of dollars annually to these lofty organizations which serve us well. Or at least it seems. The truth is many charities begin with humble and well intended purposes designed to help those less fortunate or those suffering with debilitating diseases, etc., but too many organizations have taken on huge administrative costs. It is easy to give to these organizations because they convince us that they are doing wonderful things with our donations, and many are. However, some spend nearly half of donated monies on executive pay, perks and travel expenses, building and material costs as well as fundraisers promoting their causes. Be wise about the organizations you typically donate too. Know where the money is going and keep in mind these facts listed here.

The following is a list of charity CEO pay schedules for the year 2008 according to the "Philanthropy Journal," a web based charity watchdog group. Most of the listed salaries do not include many perks and other bonus vehicles awarded to those at the helm.

According to the Journal, Boys & Girls Clubs of America's CEO earned over one million dollars in annual salary while fellow executives spent 4.3 million dollars in travel expenses, 1.6 million dollars on conferences, and $544,000 dollars in lobbying fees. And this is after the organization received millions in government funds then claimed 3.6 million dollars in losses. MADD (Mothers against Drunk Driving) took in approximately 41 million dollars in donations in 2009 while spending 21 million dollars on salaries. The CEO of MADD says it's nobody's business what he and his staff pay themselves while the American Heart Association uses over 20,000 unpaid volunteers as the CEO recieves an annual salary as seen below.

AMERICAN HEART ASSOCIATION – CEO pay $1,010,656

YMCA of HOUSTON – CEO pay $661,634

RED CROSS of AMERICA – CEO pay $565,000

ST. JUDE RESEARCH HOSPITAL – CEO pay $589,893

THE UNITED WAY – CEO pay $530,667

SUSAN G. COLEMAN FOUNDATION – CEO pay $459,406

SOCIETY of PREVENTION of CRUELTY to ANIMALS – CEO pay $473,998

WORLD VISION – CEO pay $376,799

AMERICAN CANCER SOCIETY – CEO pay $1,027,308

MAKE A WISH FOUNDATION – CEO pay $354,487

EASTER SEALS – CEO pay $565,000

MDA – CEO pay $402,732

I could go on and list three pages of these statistics and pay schedules. However, I believe or at least I hope you get the point. Corporate America has a mentality that separates the rich from the poor and that very mentality is shared by the non-profit charity world as well. You, who can barely pay your bills are paying for salaries every time you give to certain national charity groups.

The salaries listed above are the base pay for these individuals. Several actually make three times the amount shown once their total compensation package is considered. And you thought you were donating money to the actual cause and the people in need? Think again. This is not to say that much of the monies donated do not go to help needy children or the sick and injured, but my point is, once again, that the guys on top, even in the theater of charity, are managing to take more and more for themselves. Big business proponents claim that you get what you pay for and the best paid CEO's run efficient and successful programs that only a handful of gifted individuals can do. The more a CEO is paid, the better man for the job and the better run the organization. That could be another cultural misconception. The truth is any of these organizations could be operated by many skilled and talented American business people for fractions of what these current "nobles" are being paid.

Millions of small businesses in America are run every day by hard working Americans who do not have a master's degree in business but run their companies as efficiently and effectively as any Harvard business graduate. And they do it with far less than paying themselves millions of dollars annually. Some don't even have high school diplomas, but they clearly understand how to run a business in a way that includes profits, bookkeeping, human resources and other important matters of business critical for their company's survival and eventual growth. And many did it from the ground up.

There are many good causes in our country but more than that, there are many good causes right in your own back yard. Each community has needs yet we give so much beyond the borders of our cities believing that some nationally recognized corporate charity is more deserving than the locals. The truth is it is better to take care of our own communities. Many charities target the middle class which is paying for everything, and should demand a more responsible breed of charity CEOs. Jesus told us not to cast our pearls among swine. Give, always give, but know where your gifts are going when writing that check to large charity organizations and always give with a glad heart. Do your homework and give to those charities that have the least amount of monies dedicated to the corporate paycheck.

But better than that, look around your own town, your own community, and see the needs of those you live among. There are benevolent organizations right in your own area that need your help. There are local drug abuse agencies, teen pregnancy centers, homeless night shelters, local hospitals and daycare centers. Local arts and entertainment venues that use local talent as well as historical societies, medical centers and psychological centers all needing your help or your donations.

The best example of giving in the modern world is seen in the life of Mother Theresa. An Albanian born citizen of India, she began her charity work as a Catholic nun in 1948. Seeing the poverty of her native land, she began helping the poor and dying even with the doubts of the Catholic Church. Her charities continued to grow although she was staunch in her belief that all things, including charities, must remain simple or they will be corrupted by man-made systems that will channel those very charities into non-charitable coffers of corporate thinkers.

She established Missionaries of Charities in Calcutta, India, in 1950. For over 45 years she served the poor, sick, dying and orphaned while guiding the unsuspected growth of Missionaries of Charities into a world-wide charitable foundation, first throughout India then into several other countries. At the time of her death in 1997, the Missionaries of Charities had over 4,000 sisters and an associated brotherhood of over 300 members operating 610 missions in 123 countries. This included hospices and homes for people suffering with HIV/AIDS, leprosy and tuberculosis, soup kitchens, children and family counseling programs, personal helpers, orphanages and schools.

In 1979, she was awarded the Nobel Peace Prize but refused the traditional banquet to honor laureates and asked that the $192,000 in funds be given to the poor in India. She said *"Earthly rewards are only important if they are used to help the world's needy."* When asked what can be done to promote world peace she said, *"Go home and love your family."* In her Nobel lecture she said, *"Around the world, not only in poor countries, but I found the poverty of the west so much more difficult to* remove. *When I pick up a person from the street, hungry, I give him a plate of rice, a piece of bread, I have satisfied, I have removed that hunger. But, a person that is shut out, that feels unwanted, unloved, terrified, the person who has been thrown out from society – that poverty is so hurtable and so much, I find that very difficult, each one of them, she said, is Jesus in disguise."*

Her vision for helping the needy, though criticized by some humanists and other worldly thinkers, should be an inspiration to all Christians who truly understand the spirit and importance of giving. She had an old-school philosophy to keep it simple and out of the hands of worldly corporate sponges. Giving should always be about the needy, the poor, hungry and sick and others in need. If we are to give to those who would squander just a dime on themselves, then it isn't giving at all.

Every day, we come across an opportunity to give of ourselves. The opportunity can come in the simplest ways. Perhaps it is a broken down car on the side of the road, a stranded motorist. Perhaps it's a teenager walking home from school in the rain and could just use a ride. It could be a single mother who can't pay her utility bills or perhaps a shut in who needs yard work done. It could be purchasing the meal for a family in a restaurant without their knowledge or visiting someone who is lonely or isolated. Every day we are given opportunities to commit a random act of kindness if we just slow down long enough to see it.

Each Christmas we see "Angel Trees" everywhere. Names of poor children who would otherwise, not have a gift for Christmas is hung on a tree in hopes that a stranger will pick up the name and purchase that child a gift. In reality, these poor children are given anything other than what they need and that is love and care. Many foster children today are innocent victims of the worst kind of abuse and that is neglect. Most of them are born to mothers and fathers who are slaves to drug and alcohol abuse and are in prison or simply missing in action. In our consumer mindset we believe that material gifts will somehow make these children feel part of our culture of "getting" instead of "giving". These children don't need material gifts, they need us. They need love, discipline, care and some sense of normalcy in a world that deems them unimportant. They need a year round gift of love and acceptance to avoid a life-long belief that they are outcasts.

The point is giving is not only noble, but a command from God in heaven, yet giving must be continued in the simplest of ways because once giving becomes corporate and material only, then in a way it becomes stealing. God wants you to give of yourself, not through some system that would devour most of that which should go to the poor and needy that others could be provided luxuries. Giving should provide humility among the giver, not pride nor boastfulness. See the needs of others over yourself and give with a glad heart. Jesus said, "Make to yourselves friends of the mammon of unrighteousness; that, when you fall they may receive you into everlasting habitations." Perhaps then, Jesus is telling us that if we are abundant with resources that we be good stewards that it not be all about us. He is telling us to give to the fatherless and the widow and to the coffers of the church and of all those who are in need and once again to remember to keep it all in perspective in building our treasures in heaven and not in this earth.

A good friend of mine once gave me good advice. He said to live by the 10-20-70 plan. He gives 10 percent of his annual income to his church or his favorite charity. He then puts 20 percent back into his savings, paying himself first. The remaining 70 percent he uses for living expenses, taxes, etc. He also advised this process takes diligence and discipline, and one must have a solid understanding of his/her personal finances to live this way. But this is exactly the way to live according to a debt free life. Give and give generously to the poor and needy as it is our responsibility to do so, but make sure that your donations help those truly in need and not go to the coffers of the rich.

CHAPTER 18

PROVISIONS

"Again, the kingdom of heaven is like a treasure hidden in a field, which a man found and hid; and for joy over it he goes and sells all that he has and buys that field." Matt 13:84

IN AMERICA, WE HAVE devalued everything to a monetary means and that is a huge disgrace. Life is not about money, it is not about stuff, it is not about materialism, it is not about having. Christ said, "The love of money is the root of all evil." I have seen this phrase rationalized by many writers, even confessing Christians who attempt to justify their own lust for riches by explaining that Christ is telling us that the "love" of money is the root of all evil, not necessarily money itself. Subsequently, Christ tells us "It is easier for a camel to enter through the eye of the needle than for a rich man to enter the kingdom of heaven." It is difficult to rationalize that one because it's pretty straight forward.

Jesus warned that money was "unrighteous mammon". In other words, money is the most dangerous thing in the world because it can easily become the center of our lives. Men will crave it, lust it, live for it, steal for it and even kill for it but what is worse than any of that is it will become their God. Jesus knew that the more affluent people become the less they will depend on the Father in heaven.

Money then takes the allegiance of life and lures us away from the true God. That is why Jesus said it is difficult for the rich to enter the kingdom of heaven.

The problem with money is the control it seems to have over us, and having more than we need tends to corrupt us. Once a person becomes rich he tends to want more and feel more independent and self assured. It is rare that a man is ever financially satisfied with simple provisions. Without the discipline to say no, he will always want more. He will always have a love of money, a love of things not spiritual. Another serious problem with money is that it basically separates us from God. It takes us away from our spiritual goal of building up our treasures in heaven and re-directs us to build our treasures here on earth which steers us away from the spirit and toward earthly things.

J.R.R. Tolkien's trilogy, The Lord of the Rings is a perfect example of the evil in the hearts of men. The ring symbolized a power that man simply could not resist, and it caused all kinds of strife between the habitants of middle earth resulting in the manifestation of all kinds of evil, which rose up in its name to defeat that which is good. The temptation of the ring was far beyond the ability of mere man to resist. It possessed and corrupted their hearts by exploiting their own nature. So it is with money.

What our Lord is telling us is that money is a need in our culture in order that we may obtain our daily provisions, but it is in our very nature to lust money. We do so in order that we may obtain long lasting security and live without the stress of worry for our daily needs. The problem is in doing so, we sometimes create terrible situations for others by reaping riches with disregard to their needs. This is where money turns evil through the device of usury, power and influence which has no concern for human value let alone the needs of mankind. Money can easily become the basis of pride, gluttony and cruelty, especially when money becomes one's god. When a secular system loses sight of ethical means of obtaining daily provisions then that system can easily rationalize all sorts of vice as it wonders why things are so troubled.

73% of Americans claim to be Christians. That is why we tend to call America a Christian nation. Each city in America is inundated with Christian churches and has been since its founding. Millions of dollars are given in tithes and offerings each Sunday as millions of confessing Christians worship the Lord our God in the church of their own choosing all the while believing they do their part as Christians. But something isn't adding up in this Christian nation. The fruit we are yielding doesn't seem to be that sewn of Christian hands.

In 2009, 13,687,241 Americans were arrested for breaking the law according to statistics from the office of the FBI. 581,765 of those were for violent crimes against people. 15,251 murders took place in this Christian nation where "thou shall not murder" and 8,226 of those murders were committed by youths (under the age of 18). There were 21,407 forced rapes in 2009, 126,725 robberies, 421,215 aggravated assaults, 12,204 arsons, 71,355 cases of prostitution, 270,439 cases of vandalism and 17,920 cases of embezzlement in this Christian nation. 1,440,409 people were arrested in 2009 for driving while under the influence. 594,300 were arrested for drunkenness and 1,663,582 for drug abuse violations. In 2009, there were 93,434 runaways reported in this Christian nation of plenty.

By the 8th grade, 52 percent of American students will have tried alcohol. 41 percent will try cigarettes and at least 20 percent will try marijuana. In one day in this Christian nation, 4,210 teens will contract a sexually transmitted disease. 3,610 will be assaulted, 80 will be raped, and 2,861 will drop out of school. 1,377 will become teen mothers and 1,106 will get an abortion. 1,000 teens will begin drinking, 500 will start doing drugs, 420 will be arrested for drug use and 6 will die from suicide, all in one day in this Christian nation. 37,000 teens will die this year. 30 percent will be in automobile accidents, and many of those will involve high speeds, drugs and alcohol. The average age for sexually active teens is now 16, and Ritalin is the new gateway drug for this daycare generation.

In this Christian nation, there are approximately 2,019,230 Americans currently in prison, and last year 42 of them were executed for their acts of heinous crimes against people. 92 percent of those incarcerated today are in prison because of some crime related to drug or alcohol abuse. 37,000 Americans will die on the highway this year with 14,000 of those related to people driving under the influence of alcohol or drugs. Since 2007, over 46,000 people have died in Mexico's drug war because of America's insatiable drug market. Every year, nearly 20,000 Americans die from drug overdoses in this Christian nation. We make up only 2 percent of the world's population yet are responsible for over 50 percent of illicit drug use.

Approximately 34,000 people died in 2009 due to suicide, with men committing four times that of women. Suicide is the third leading cause of death in teenagers and a serious problem in the elderly population. 12,100 people died of alcoholism or health issues closely related to alcoholism. 30.6 percent of America is now considered obese in this Christian nation where 1,210,000 abortions take place annually proving that the most dangerous place for an American child is in the womb. The average professing Christian rarely reads the Bible but watches approximately 28 hours of television a week. In that week he/she will be exposed to thousands of images of sexuality and violence as will their children.

The pornography business in this Christian nation is the leading entertainment venue taking approximately 12 billion dollars annually with thousands of young men and women lining up to perform sexual acts on camera. Thousands of Americans, both male and female are now addicted to porn. Human trafficking has become a huge problem across this country as thousands of poor and unprotected immigrants are exploited by coyotes and other criminal elements that leverage fear and intimidation upon unsuspecting people trying to make a better life for themselves. Thousands of young immigrant women are forced into prostitution in this Christian nation each year convinced that there is nowhere to turn for help.

In a true Christian nation, the Church would have proper influence to help the less fortunate, to act as a buffer between the wolves of the health care industry and the sick. It would heavily influence education which would continue the historic scriptural lessons that created a national moral standard against immorality and criminal behavior resulting in a strong and independent people, and it would be expressed and respected in the arts as it once was. But, we are not a Christian nation. This charge does not set well with many people. Let me explain. We are rather a consumer nation and the dollar of commerce is our god. Corporate monetary rules are our bible and immorality our way of life. The statistics simply do not lie.

Over 100 years of a secular designed education system is taking its toll. This humanistic system really began picking up speed by the 1970s, teaching that nothing in life matters more than the self. Our monetary system is but a reflection of the ideology of self indulgence, gluttony, corruption and hedonism. Our personal debt is but a reflection of self indulgence as well.

Christ said *"No servant can serve two masters, for either he will hate the one and love the other, or he will be loyal to one and despise the other."* God or even the idea of God is despised by the secularist ruling class of this country. In science, education, the arts, modern philosophy, in our monetary systems and in government, God is no longer allowed as the sovereign creator of the universe. He is no longer accepted as the moral authority in our post-modern society. He is now publicly "offensive" to our mainstream humanist culture, which are small in numbers but powerful in influence, especially in the field of education and cultural philosophies. A new world of humanistic bullies have taken hold and "Political Correctness." their tool of choice, has taught a generation of Americans that we are not to invite God into our public and professional lives and to do so should be illegal or by the very least, inappropriate.

This is not to say that there are no Christians in the United States. There are millions of Christians, or at least confessing Christians. However, real Christians are those understanding the practice of a discipleship of Christ. To understand what a disciple is, we must understand how to die to ourselves. Christ said, *"If you are to live, you must die"* . . . but many do not understand nor practice that concept as a part of their faith. Having a little fish emblem on the back of your $50,000 automobile may not be an exclusive passage into the Kingdom of Heaven. Christ said, *"You will know them by their fruit."* That pretty much sums it up. Debt is a fruit of our making and is a sin. Perhaps, it may be better to be poor than a fat man in the eye of the needle.

Even in the Protestant church today, sermons on tithing outweigh all others as the need for money is in constant demand. Perhaps attempting to operate a "spiritual entity" via secular business principles is a conflict of spiritual interest. Our church buildings were once opened to the general public as sanctuaries. Now, they remain locked so thieves will not break in to steal the expensive sound systems and other things of worldly monetary value. Even the Church has gone the way of the dollar as many religious affiliations in America buy up property and own real estate worth millions as people live homeless and go hungry around them.

Televangelism has exploded in the last twenty years raking in billions of dollars for prophets of profit ready to pray for your soul as they steal your last dollar. The health and wealth industry of the emerging church and the prosperity gospels continue to entertain the masses with humanistic ideologies that preach personal happiness and success as the fulcrum of God's existence as if He were here to serve us. In other words, it's all about me. Apostasy is rampant because of the infiltration of money and self indulgence and its influence in the modern American church.

My point is not to make good folks feel bad for being successful, nor to disrespect the Church but rather to place things in proper perspective. God is not about money. It has nothing to do with his kingdom on earth, Jesus makes that quite clear. That is almost impossible for people of the wealthiest nation on earth to understand. He never said, "Thou shalt go unto the earth and build a mega-church and live in mansions paid for with the profits made from My Word and by all means be happy and prosperous." Life just isn't going to be happy and prosperous. It is difficult and full of sorrow and want for most of the people on earth. God charges us to give of ourselves to ease these natural burdens on others. Take a look at the Disciples of Christ. All but one died horrible deaths in His name. Thousands of Christians were killed in sporting events that entertained Roman citizens while hundreds of thousands of others have been martyred because they refused to denounce their faith. Even today, we read of Christians around the world that are singled out and killed because of their belief in Christ, especially in Islamic regions. The Bible is considered old and outdated by modern thinkers and philosophers who despise any thought of a God in heaven that would require any form of sacrifice of the self.

It is one thing for Christian churches and organizations to respond with help and money to a place that has been devastated by a terrible storm, but it is a totally different situation if the same city were hit with a terrible plague that was taking thousands of lives. How many professing modern Christians would respond to that city to help take care of the sick at the risk of losing their own lives? Perhaps this is a question each confessing Christian needs to ask him or herself. What if Christ demanded that all Christian teachers stop teaching evolution to young children in today's school system? What if he demanded that we pray to our Christian God in the school halls despite the consequences? How many would really sacrifice their job for the word of God? Actually, these are the very things Christ demands from his followers.

Many churches today have done Christians a huge disservice by trying to make us feel good about ourselves. Christianity is difficult, plain and simple. Christ said to follow Him we must pick up and carry our cross. If we truly follow Him, we will suffer terrible things. The world will hate us and prosecute us. It will think we are crazy and out of touch with reality, yet it will have nothing to offer up but deception such as a debt filled life.

The only time we see Jesus become violent was when he chased the money-changers from the temple. In those times, many Jews were still practicing animal sacrifices. People would come to the temple to make sacrificial blood offerings. In order to do so, one had to trade Roman coin with Jewish to make purchases of sacrificial animals and the money-changers bought and sold those coins for profit. The belief was that the larger the sacrifice, the larger the blessing. So, other merchants brought cattle and various animals including doves for the poor to be purchased by those making sacrifices at the temple. Christ, who seriously opposed such practices was outraged because the temple of God had been tarnished with commerce. He fashioned a whip out of a reed and violently attacked the money-changers and merchants, throwing over their tables and expelling them from the house of worship. *"This is my Father's house yet you have turned it into a den of thieves."* This country was built on the basis of the Christian-Judeo faith but mighty bankers and industrialists have turned it into a den of thieves through corporatism and the practice of usury and mass consumerism.

Christ practiced scarcity. He told us again and again not to worry about things of monetary value and warned us of placing our trust in such objects of idolatry. He specifically instructed his followers not to place their lives and faith into monetary means of this earth which thieves can steal, yet place all things in faith of the Father in heaven. Christians are to live in the spirit, not in the world. Modern Christians must come to terms with who they really wish to worship, the God of this world through monetary means and comforts which result in debt or the God of Heaven through a life of discipleship, discipline, spiritual growth and sacrifice which results in freedom by living a debt free life and within one's means and obedient to the Lord.

Our financial situation is in direct correlation with our spiritual selves. *"As a man thinks in his heart, so is he."* As I mentioned earlier, your checkbook (or your credit card statement) is an excellent reminder of where your heart is. Everything about you can be expressed through how you spend your money. We can spend every day of our lives collecting material goods and yet remain completely empty. Steel Magnate Andrew Carnegie spent his entire life making money and became one of the wealthiest men in American history. He woke up one day and realized that he had more money than anyone yet he was completely empty inside. He spent the rest of his life giving most of it away.

Never before in modern times has a culture had so much yet been as empty and unhappy as ours. Depression is widespread as Prosaic and Xanax sales are off the charts. I have heard we are suffering from afluenza. Easy credit and debt have given Americans an appearance of wealth, and we are avoiding all kinds of emotional pain through spending. The avoidance of natural emotional pain creates depression on a wide scale and has resulted in a culture of addiction.

Materialism keeps us depressed by keeping us from natural daily grieving and takes away our archetypical needs (family, parents and relationships) and replaces Grandma with a Play Station II. When you have less, you have to live within your archetype - father, mother, family, etc. Affluence takes these away and replaces them with materialism that cannot converse, lacks a heartbeat and leaves us completely alone. And with the bombardment of commercialism we become more self-driven. This has lead to a significant rise of drug use and suicide as well as dependence on governmental programs and other socialist ideologies. We feel a huge hole inside and try to fill it with all kinds of things like drugs, shopping, pornography, sports, alcohol, bad relationships, and various other means of immorality. We have listened to the lies of the materialistic and social oligarchs that have enslaved us for their benefit. Life is not about money. It's about God, about family, about community and this gives us hope and redirection to find it's all about love.

Love is what Christ's whole message was about, how to love our fellow man, how to find the needs of others as important and in some cases, more important than our own. We are to find our significance in the Father and practice our love for all mankind daily. He taught us his view of love which is to sacrifice for the betterment of oneself or for the betterment of others, mainly our family, our spouse, our children, and our neighbor. We achieve this through sacrifice, the sacrifice of telling ourselves no. Our world, however, tells us we can have whatever we want as we are bombarded daily with materialism all the while snaring us into the pits of debt.

Our God is a mystery. We see what we know of Him through His creation and His word. One thing we do know is He is a God of order. He has created a universe of order and one with strict consequences if we stray from that order. If we steal, cheat, lie, have an affair on our spouse, become gluttonous, murder, lust, etc., there are serious consequences and sooner or later we pay for our choices. This is regardless of whether a person chooses to believe in Him or not . . . the rules remain the same. The same holds true for us financially. If we think we are going to break these rules, whether we are ignorant of them or not, we are sadly mistaken. If you purchase goods, you must pay. If you do not, you will pay by some other method but you will pay. We are to pay for what we purchase. Christ said, *"Give unto Caesar that which is Caesar's but give to God that which is God's."* This means pay your taxes, your bills, your promissory notes and any other financial transactions you have. Pay cash for things you need and if you can't, then DO NOT BUY THEM. This is a very simple mathematical situation. If you do not have money for an expensive car, do not buy it, especially on a six year note. If you do not have money for a big house, buy a small house. If you can't afford a vacation or new clothes, do not purchase them with a credit card. Remember how God's laws work. Debt is the result of having things you cannot afford, and there are serious consequences for that.

Many people have purchased things they cannot afford in order to deal with emotional and psychological issues in their lives. They may have grown up poor and ashamed so the first thing they do is surround themselves with things that they believe will take away those humble reminders of the pain of not having. For me, being poor meant having little choices and being trapped in ignorance and want with no way out. I thought having stuff would make me forget all that. Once I had things on credit, I just became a liar. I was avoiding me in order to be like the folks next door, all the while not knowing they were doing the same to be like me. God has a way of reminding us who we are. I, too, had to learn that stuff will never bring the joy that is found in the Word of God, a loving family and the simplicities of life. That acceptance through discipline gave me real freedom from ignorance, want and poverty. God showed me that my poorness was never keeping me from loving or being loved.

During WWII, Dr. Victor Frankl, a prominent psychiatrist from Vienna had the misfortune to find himself a guest of the 3rd Reich at the notorious Auschwitz concentration camp. He recognized the horror of the camp upon arrival and soon found himself and his family hoarded like cattle from the train cars into lines separating first, men and women then by ages and abilities. That was the last time he ever saw his beloved wife, brother, father and mother. He was then deprived of the small amount of belongings he'd carried with him. Within a few hours he was stripped of his personal clothing and moved to a large delousing area and then given filthy striped clothing that had the putrid smell of the previous owner who had most likely been worked to death.

As the months went by he found survival in the camp to be almost impossible physically and emotionally yet through the horrid conditions he found a small number of men, including himself, who were able to transcend the animal like existence that they had been lowered to. He found these men had one thing in common and that was faith. With all he had been through he discovered that it was a deep sense of faith that kept this small group from losing any form of human dignity they had left. These were the group of men who would still give their last portion of bread ration to another suffering soul.

He also found that human suffering is a part of life itself. He said, "To suffer is human". Once everything had been taken from him, his family, his belongings, his clothing, his position, his profession, his dignity and his self respect he found himself truly naked before God and through this experience he found that we have absolutely no control over anything but our attitude and through our suffering we may find ourselves closer to God than at any other time in our lives. "To live is to suffer. To survive is to find meaning in that suffering". Perhaps that is what Jesus has been trying to tell us all along. The love Christ tried to teach us, the kind of love that transcends all things including loss, time and even death. The love that reaches out to comfort others at sacrifice to itself is the love of Christ. This kind of love needs little provisions to exist.

We must have provisions to survive but thanks to easy credit, most Americans are living way beyond their means and beyond their daily provisional needs and many Christians have found themselves trapped in the pits of debt by following worldly desires. Let perpetual debt be someone else's problem, not yours. It is a sin to be in debt, and the fiscal consequences of that sin are painful for everyone as it muffles the voice of the Holy Spirit. God did not design mankind to live that way. For the good graces of men in England and the United States in the former century did away with slavery through great strife and national tragedy that all Americans should be free. The banksters have unfortunately created a new form of slavery for all men. This new form of slavery is just as evil, if not worse. Debt free is freedom and allows Christians the ability to spread God's kingdom on earth.

Becoming debt free will take discipline and remember, discipline is the closest to God we will ever be on this planet. The bottom line is we must learn to be happy with less. Scarcity is your sword against the armies of the banks and gaining the discipline to say no to yourself is paramount. Our expanded standard of living in the last forty years has created our prison. Perhaps it's time for you to really take up your cross and follow Jesus.

CHAPTER 19

TRUTH IN A CRAZY WORLD

"Finally my brethren, be strong in the Lord and in the power of his might. Put on the whole armor of God that you may be able to stand against the wiles of the devil. For we do not struggle against flesh and blood, but against principalities, against powers, against the rulers of this present darkness, against spiritual hosts of wickedness in the heavenly places; therefore, take up the whole armor of God that you may be able to withstand the evil day, and having done all, to stand." . . . *Eph 6:9*

I HOPE BY NOW you have some idea how all your debt came about. It didn't just happen. The banking system through the process of usury produces nothing, yet makes two to four times in profit compared to the value of a product to be paid back by the borrower. As you have learned, this is done through debt interest created out of nothing. These profits are resulting in the purchase of power over people. This beastly system if allowed to continue unchecked will indirectly control everyone through purchase and influence. As previously mentioned, we may come to a point where we will not be allowed to work, eat, purchase, etc., without the permission of this system. The oppressive system is much larger than just you and I, and it is setting the nations up for a new world order in which America will simply be one of its servants.

Imagine, you have a mortgage . . . look around. That means the chances of everyone else in your neighborhood having one too is a pretty sure thing. All the other homes, the factories, the high rises, hotels, airports, farms, convenience stores, shopping malls, apartment buildings, fast food restaurants, etc. You can only imagine the avalanche of money flowing into the banking complex. This is money that should be going to small business owners, factories, farmers, ranchers, manufacturers or those who produce and create. Unfortunately, the beast has rerouted it all to the financial institutions of the world.

So, what are the banks doing with all that wealth? They are spending it, but not on pleasures. Once a person has spent so much on the pleasures of life, he must find other interests and that interest is power and control. Without succumbing to paranoia I will take the liberty here to say they are acquiring power and control over you, me, and our children. They are buying up people, groups and institutions. They have massive influence over our leaders, political parties, TV and media outlets, the Internet, cable networks, newspapers, magazines, publishers, wire services, motion picture studios, universities, labor unions, churches, trade associations, tax exempt foundations, multi-national corporations, and even over what you say in public or in the workplace. What we are seeing come to fruition didn't just happen over the last couple of years. This system has been in the works for several generations.

"Capital must protect itself in every possible way, both by combination and legislation. Debts must be collected, mortgages foreclosed as rapidly as possible. When through the process of law the common people lose their homes, they will become more docile and more easily governed through the strong arm of government applied by a central power of wealth under leading financiers. These truths are well

> *known among our principal men who are now engaged
> in forming imperialism to govern the world. By dividing
> the voters through the political party system we can get
> them to expend their energies in fighting for questions of
> no importance. It is thus by discreet action we can secure
> for ourselves that which has been so well planned and
> so successfully accomplished."* US Banker Association
> Magazine – 1924

This has been going on not only in America but in all industrialized nations. The Third World has already been taken over by the BEAST via monies routed through the UN giving political funding to politicians building totalitarian systems. Through the International Monetary Fund created by the UN, International Bankers are moving toward a worldwide system of financial slavery through their device of usury. The International Monetary Fund could be the beginning of a world bank through a new world system of socialism or humanistic philosophical values in education, politics, finances, and even religion while guised as a world humanitarian organization where Christianity will not be tolerated.

The UN is made up of all kinds of dictators and worldly banking and industrial organizations such as the Trilateral Commission and the Bilderberg group. The Trilateral Commission, created by David Rockefeller, Chase-Manhattan Bank Chairman, formed this group in 1973, made up of powerful bankers, industrialists, etc. Current members include Alan Greenspan, George H. Bush, Henry Kissinger, Jimmy Carter, Bill Clinton, etc. (The group only has 300 members) and was originally created to foster better financial and industrial relations between the US, Europe and Japan. In 1954, The Bilderberg Group was created with a special invitation of 140 powerful people who meet annually to discuss world problems and hash out other issues in total secrecy. Why would a very select group of powerful and wealthy people get together once a year anyway unless they have some kind of concerted agenda. These are very busy folks who aren't getting together simply to throw business ideas around over a good cigar and a bottle of fine brandy. They have an agenda which doesn't include your problems.

Other UN based groups such as League of Nations and the Council on Foreign Relations are other worldly government organizations who believe that national sovereignties and western capitalism are a threat to world socialist agendas.

President John F. Kennedy warned us of these secret societies, and President Dwight Eisenhower called the society of power or shadow world government "The Military Industrial Complex". He warned us in the 1950's that something was engulfing the world; "Something that demands our whole attention, absorbs our entire beings. We face a hostile ideology, global in scope, atheistic in character, ruthless in purpose and insidious in method. The dangers it poses promises to be of indefinite duration." These financial and political powers own the media and understand quite well human sociology and psychology to keep the masses entertained with issues that don't really matter, such as inundating the public with the lifestyles of celebrities as if such information is important, or creating an obsession with sports and sex through mass commercialism. They know to have America addicted to unimportant things like television, the lives of celebrities, and continuous gluttonous consumption while constantly worrying about our monthly payments will keep us completely apathetic about such boring and uninteresting issues that deal with world banking, social and political systems.

Our old enemy socialism is definite and cunning and very much alive and well, but what has that got to do with personal finances? Very much actually! Just go back and read the very first quote in the introduction. The first step in any socialistic plan is the reform of capitalism, especially at a time when capitalism appears to be broke. When the capitalist system is neutralized, then the rest of the socialistic ideology comes easy. The first step to an efficient plan is a socialist and atheistic takeover of the entire education system which was accomplished in the United States by the great secularist John Dewey in the early part of the 20th century. The second step to capitalist neutralization is control over the money supply which requires a central bank along with a fiat monetary system. That was accomplished with the advent of the Federal Reserve in 1913. Major controls over infrastructure and services must also be obtained. That was accomplished through President Roosevelt's New Deal in 1933. Now, we have seen another great surge toward socialism in the last two years as the government takes over more free enterprise systems and creates more and more dependence upon the state than Americans have ever had as the Marxist ideologies of social engineering of the 1960s and 1970s come to fruition.

Karl Marx theorized that a capitalist society would never be able to sustain or continue its ideology as the upper crest mentality would sooner or later abuse the masses to the point that the working class would violently revolt and create a socialist society throughout the world. Does this mean a nation of faith which results in freedom could be reduced to a land of suppression of liberties such as free speech and freedom of religion? Absolutely, once a successful system such as capitalism is hijacked and perverted by a small class of schemers at the top, then it is easy to make that very system appear to be a wicked enemy of the people and socialism will be there to pick up the pieces. We are seeing how well that is working as we view the leftist demonstrators picketing Wall Street for many of the wrong reasons.

The neo-world socialists understood that a revolution by the working class in America would be utterly impossible because of our cultural influence of Christian values but a subversive campaign over time could easily manipulate the masses through support of the very system that would eventually lead to the downfall. The first step of this infiltration of social manipulation is a challenge to free speech called "political correctness" and works by creating an attitudinal atmosphere where certain aspects of verbal expression are villianized, especially language that would not promote the evolution of the human spirit and tolerance of leftist thought and agendas and must be cast out of popular mainstream dogma (Christianity is of course, exempt from humanistic tolerance). Political correctness is another philosophy that didn't just evolve from the bowels of the literate left in America. It has been purposely designed by those who have infiltrated the west with nonsense designed to undermine our very liberties of free speech. Before you think me some conspiracy theorist, allow me to explain.

In 1917, Marxist Vladimir Lenin returned to his beloved land of Russia to further spew his vixen within the violent Bolshevik uprising against the ruling class leading to a humanistic society based in socialism. The struggle led to the deaths of millions of Russians and set up the bloodiest conflicts in human history, which would culminate in the death of millions of people worldwide throughout the 20th century. This socialist rhetoric based on the writings of Karl Marx, was popularized in Germany by the 1920s. At that time, Germany was in political chaos because of the military demise of WWI, and many political groups were vying for power including the Communists (or socialists). A group of political social activists set up a "Think-Tank" for Marxist thought modeled after the writings of Marx and Engels at Frankfurt University holding its first "school of theory" in 1922.

A character named Gerig Lutkosh was part of the original group in Germany and his writings on culture would become the basis of the school as he translated the theory from political to cultural terms, resulting in the idea of "political correctness." Max Horkheimer became the school leader. He believed, while recognizing the capitalist success of the west that revolution would not come from the working class. This form of socialism is known as Fabian Socialism, meaning communism via evolution instead of revolution. This same form of socialism was also preached by Saul Alinsky in his book <u>Rules for Radicals</u>. His book, which is dedicated to the greatest radical in recorded history, Lucifer, among others, was embraced by the radical left created from the leftovers of the American Cultural Revolution. Alinsky published his <u>Rules for Radicals</u> in 1971 for the specific purpose of harnessing the unfocused chaotic discontent of the 1960s youth rebellion into a long term tool for the destruction of the current American system from the inside out. His goal was to produce a generation of "Realistic Radicals" who would worm their way into our churches, our government, our schools, our businesses, our labor unions and our media. Now almost 40 years later, our current government administration and an impressive liberal left ideology in America represent the successful culmination of the Alinsky process of social revolution.

> *"Back in 1927, an American socialist by the name of Norman Thomas, six times candidate for President under the socialist ticket said, The American people would never vote for a socialist, but under the name of Liberalism, the American people will adopt every fragment of the socialist program."* Ronald Reagan

As for the students of the School for Marxist thought, they clearly understood that they would have to find other avenues in which to lay the seeds of socialism in the west; however, they were expelled from Germany in 1933 by Adolf Hitler who had come to despise socialist communism. Most of the school was transferred to New York City, and made their home at Columbia University, and later found that "other avenue" through the American education system. Once in America, it shifted its aim of despising German society to despising American society. In 1950, one of the school leaders, Theodore Ordorno wrote, "Many Americans obtain fascist traits and therefore are mentally or emotionally imbalanced and should have some kind of sensitivity training," setting the stage for classes in cultural diversity as well as other demeaning social engineered systems among mainstream America.

Though the bulk of the school returned to Frankfurt University in 1946, it had laid serious groundwork for the development for Marxist thinking upon the American university system. This Fabian system solidified during the 1960s by manipulating and exploiting the American under classes and minorities by perverting our interpretation of freedom by devaluing self-responsibility which continues today throughout our education system. Political correctness is simply a form of cultural control to suppress freedom of speech and religion, especially Christianity, to undermine public opinion, to weaken the defense of free people and to re-educate school children through methods of historical revisionism and atheistic ideologies disguised as scientific data yet heavy in humanistic post-modern and atheistic rhetoric and thought. It is a socialist manifestation upon the shores of America, and it's working very well. Most Americans are clueless that it even exists, especially mainstream educators and teachers who profess the Christian faith but teach anti-Christian philosophies.

Political correctness shuts down debate with topics that are disagreeable to its agenda. This can be done by labeling the offender with terms or phrases that color that person a social enemy. Popular political correct terms such as racist, right-wing, fanatic, religious nut-job, bigot, prejudice, Nazi, Fascist, etc, are common to this subjection to anyone who disagrees with the political correct dogma. Political correct proponents avoid the issues such as moral degeneracy as they support phrases including multi-culturalism, diversity, sensitivity training, and social programming, all which divide us as a nation rather than unite us. They make it a point to shut down debate if they are opposed, particularly in the media and education especially if they can label their opponent with popular political correct names such as those listed above. If you can control the language, you can control the argument. Most Americans verbally disagree with any form of political correctness yet have absorbed it as it is seen in every aspect of American life. Don't believe me? Just send out an email at work that mentions your faith in God through a belief in his son Christ Jesus and see what happens.

The concept of political correctness gives way to the birth of historical revisionism. In 1620, the Mayflower sailed from Holland (not England, they left England ten years prior for Holland) westward to the new world. Dr. Dale Tacket in Focus on the Family's Truth Project reports of an American classroom textbook that mentions the historic journey, and even goes so far to repeat the inscription left by those brave Pilgrims at Plymouth Rock, "We whose names are underwritten . . . have undertaken a voyage to plant the first colony." The problem, as Dr. Tacket points out, is that is not exactly what is written. The real inscription reads, "In the name of God, amen. We whose names are underwritten . . . have undertaken, for the glory of God, an advancement of the Christian faith, a voyage to plant the first colony." Such revisionism, Dr. Tacket points out, has taken place in classrooms all over America in the last 50 years.

Recently we have seen changes in classic American literature to go so far to protect people from being offended by changing wording in classic books such as <u>Tom Sawyer</u>. I wonder what Mark Twain would think of the climate of revisionism in modern times? Karl Marx went on to say, "If I can change your historical context, I can change the way you view the present." There is an extreme left ideology behind historical revisionism in our current education system. Marx continued, "If you can change what people believe about their pasts, you can control what they think about in the future."

Political correctness was born out of the notion that no culture could be worse than the western culture or civilization. Its idea teaches that homophobia (another political correct term), racism, slavery, etc., is unique to the West, ignoring historical facts of every other culture in time, many which were extremely barbaric without a hint of human rights. In American history school books today the most villainous display of cruelty to mankind is not the Vikings, nor the Nazis, nor is it the Romans, the Barbarians or Huns or the Turks. Rather it is the American born KKK. Bad guys in their own right I assure you. Yet historically, they don't even rank on the scale of evil that has perpetuated mankind over the last 2,000 years. Attila the Hun wiped out thousands of lives just to watch people die. The Russians alone killed millions of their own people through the advent of communism in the 20ᵗʰ century at the hands of leaders such as Lenin and Stalin, yet not a lot of stink is made of it by those who write and edit our children's learned curriculum. The point is to make us feel bad about who we are and how we got here.

Recently, I had to attend a class on Cultural Diversity which is required by one of the state agencies where I carry a commission for continuing education credit. The class was interesting, not from a learning standpoint but from a deception standpoint. Half of the class was dedicated to the understanding of the Islamic religion. I found this contradictory, as any other religion would have been shunned profusely. No secular class in America today would even consider a half day of study dedicated to the understanding Christianity. The ACLU and other atheist and socialist organizations would have a cow. Cultural diversity is a dividing tool that has had the adverse affect upon our culture than some unwittingly intended. Instead of bringing people together it is a device that separates cultures and demonizes traditional American values and cultures, especially Christians. It would be better that we taught unity rather than diversity where our nation is concerned and an acceptance of Christianity as a religion that many take seriously and as a way of everyday life.

As Americans we throw the word "democracy" around a lot and those at the top love to use it in justifying their political ambitions to a voting public. Actually, America was never intended to be a democracy, per sae, and several founding fathers warned of such. The word "democracy" really wasn't used in our national dogma until around the beginning of the 1900's. This country, in the minds of most of the founding fathers, was designed to be a "republic." The difference is simple. A democracy is a government designed by the vote of the people to obtain what they want politically or simply put, mob rule! But a republic is a system designed with set laws which govern a free people in a way that disallows corruption through the foundation of and respect for the law and a balance of powers at the top through a tri-tier system. A republic also ignores special interests and considers individuality the mainstay of the foundation of human rights through the written law, not case law or laws appointed by the magistrate that would protect certain groups within the republic or specified groups favored by certain political or cultural sympathies of those with political powers.

"Sir, what did you give us?" asked a woman at Benjamin Franklin's retirement ceremony, in which he replied, "A republic Madam, if you will keep it."

Several of the framers of the Constitution and the Declaration of Independence knew that a democracy would give a people some of the worst of government waste. James Madison said, *"Democracies have ever been found incompatible with personal securities or the rights of prosperity and have in general been short in their lives as they have been violent in their deaths."* Alexander Hamilton added, *"Our founders never wanted a Democracy."* John Adams said, *"Remember, democracy never lasts long. It soon wastes, exhausts, and murders itself. There never was a democracy yet that did not commit suicide."* This is news to all of us as we have always been taught in school that we live in a democracy.

Basically, there are five types of rule on this planet. First, there are monarchies, which are dictatorships or rule by one. In reality, no one person really rules anything. Even Adolf Hitler had an inner circle of men who influenced many of his decisions. It really is a rule by a group, so we can honestly say that true monarchs do not exist on earth. Secondly, we have oligarchies which are rule by the few. This is the most common sense of ruler-ship in the world today. Then, we have anarchy which means rule by no one. This is silly, because this is a temporary form of government or lack thereof that will not last. Sooner or later someone will convince all the others that he is the answer to their terrible situation and will quickly rise to the top as leader. We have established leadership by one really doesn't exist, so it will become an oligarch. Then we have a democracy meaning rule by the majority. Strange, as this word in Russian means "Bolshevik," but I digress. The problem with democracy means the wants and desires of the masses cannot be restrained, and once the majority of people want everything (this is where we are today), the system collapses. Finally, we have a republic which means rule by law. The law is to keep the land honest. The rights of the individual are not governed by the majority but by the law. A law recognized by man that there exists a supreme dominating creator who has given specific rights to every man, woman, and child. Those rights are not man-made yet God made. That is the basis of the law.

That law is based on the ten commandments of the Christian/ Judeo teachings and is not rule set forth by God. Rather it is the reflection of the nature of God, a supreme creator of all things and in him are given our rights as men. Through such, justice is found for all.

The Bill of Rights is law. The US Constitution is law. Our country was designed to be a republic but not necessarily a democracy. Like the laws of God, certain rules apply and ignorance and disrespect of those laws can result in serious consequences. Our republic is supposed to work the same way. Ignorance and disrespect of our laws which lay the foundation for ethics will have consequences for all of us. Unregulated banking practices and corrupt corporate operations were not to be allowed under the laws of the republic yet they have flourished under the concepts of corporate hijacked democracy. A federal reserve bank which has resulted in a system run by cut-throat international bankers was never to be allowed under our laws of the republic either.

> *"Our Constitution was made only for a moral and religious people. It is wholly inadequate to the government of any other."* . . . John Adams

So, what is truth? I have been told by many modern day philosophers and teachers that truth is relative. Relativism is a Post Modern idea. This post-modern idea means that my truth is my truth and your truth is your truth based on cultural thinking perceived by self-serving attitudes. This is typical of a culture that doesn't want to respect a moral authority. That sounds typical of modern thinkers who do everything they can to avoid consequences, but it is a down-right lie. Ultimate truth exists. There is ultimate truth in this universe and we see it expressed in God's laws of nature and his very word. There is a moral authority in this universe. Attempting to live the lie of ignoring that fact will have consequences. Living in debt is living that lie.

Christ gave the exact answer for all truth. He said, *"For this reason I came and for this reason I was born, as a testament to the truth."* That truth can only be found in the knowledge of the Father, the Son and the Holy Spirit. That acceptance will bring us grace and in that we find our true emotional intelligence through humility.

So, is our culture telling us lies? Yes, every hour of every day, and we believe those lies because we want to. They appeal to our nature and our ego. This is how we are lied to socially and economically because the lies appeal to our desires so we believe. It is natural for us to want to believe that we live in a world where we can trust our leaders and our culture to tell the truth. Unfortunately it just doesn't work that way.

Jesus says *"I tell you the truth"* at least 75 times in the Gospels. But it is our nature to suppress truth, to distort it, to color it, to reject it and follow evil or simply exchange the truth for lies. A constant battle rages for our minds. The beginning of the cosmic battle began with Adam and Eve. The truth on one side, the lie on the other, and we are in the middle with the freedom to choose which we want for our lives. God gives us the truth but he does not force us to take it. Lies are deeply powerful and can lead us to believe the most insane things. Our very nature is inclined to choose the lies over the truth. It is easy to believe the lie. Debt is a lie! Life without debt is the truth!

CONCLUSION

We live in a country that has benefitted well because of a free world market of trade. This system created the greatest and most prosperous country in the world because the average person was free to participate in the American idea and reap the benefits of his God given talents. Unfortunately, our remarkable capitalist system has been kidnapped by world dominating robber barons leaving us slaves by using our own ideologies against us in their attempt at world domination. As if guided by unseen powers, they are tightening their grips on all Americans through financial, social and political gains manipulated through a public that has lost its dependence and respect of a Holy God.

We live in a country blessed with an abundance of natural resources tapped into by generations of people who understood the value of unlimited opportunities to reap from those resources through hard work, sacrifice, and determination with respect of the creator of that abundance. But, perhaps prosperity has become our downfall. We have raised a generation that is not familiar with the hard work and discipline it takes to maintain such a culture and the creation of easy debt has resulted in slavery of a people. Most take for granted the massive work and technology behind the workings to simply run one's I-phone. They are completely ignorant of the process it takes to drill and refine the gasoline that conveniently powers our automobiles to take us from point a to point b in relative comfort and ease. Have we forgotten the struggles and sacrifices of those who came before us? What of this brave new world?

To borrow from Bradbury, "Something wicked this way comes" and yes Junior, there really are things that go bump in the night. There is an invisible domain in which angels and demons fight over souls in vast array. This idea is foolishness to worldly thinkers but regardless, the battle rages. The battle is for your mind, your soul, your very being. This cosmic battle has been underway throughout time and you are a participant, believe it or not. You will be influenced naturally by evil for we are all born into sin and the human heart is wicked and cannot be trusted. You will be influenced by good through acceptance, study and the discipline of God's word and the life, death, and resurrection of Christ Jesus. This is truth and in such is found redemption and salvation.

Contrary to worldly thinking, good and evil are not polar opposites. Evil is not omnipresent. Evil is not the opposite of good, rather the perversion of it. A tooth is good, tooth decay is evil, but the tooth was good before the decay. This is a mystery and one we will not understand until we pass from this troubled world. But, it remains a fact.

Man was created as good in the likeness of God but the evil one corrupted man by separating him from his creator through pride. Think of it this way. There is no such thing as cold, only an absence of warmth and evil can only thrive where there is an absence of God. That absence is found where men deny God's truth as we have seen come to fruition in America over the last century. World philosophies operate in a constant state of darkness, for Satan is the god of this age. Therefore, deceit is everywhere, and we are being deceived daily.

Our only hope is to be washed in the blood of the Lamb, to be knighted into the heavenly battle, so to speak, by believing Christ is the true Savior of this world through his death on the cross and his ultimate resurrection. As knights we become part of the royal family of the Lord of lords and understand that while on this earth, we will participate in the foregoing battle for mankind. Like any soldier, we must know our enemy and his cunning, his spies, his ideologies, his weaponry and his army and be on constant guard. We must train daily and always be vigilant in the word of God and the worthiness of our knighthood. We must be brave.

> *"Stand therefore, having girded your loins with truth, having put on the breastplate of righteousness, and having shod your feet with the preparation of the gospel of peace, and above all, taking the shield of faith with which you will be able to quench all the fiery arrows of the wicked one and take the helmet of salvation and the sword of the Spirit which is the Word of God; praying always with all prayer and supplication in the spirit, being watchful to this end with all perseverance and supplication for all the saints."*
> Ephesians 6: 10-18

Many good Christian people are lost in this world of secular deceit because we are no longer taught a Christian world view. Many people believe, even some professing Christians that religious expression should only be exemplified on Sunday morning and should never be allowed into daily life. This is completely at odds with a Christian world view. It is one thing to believe in God, "for even the demons believe", but Christ demands that we be disciples.

Christians must live and practice what they preach daily as commanded in the Gospels of Christ. We must believe in the historical resurrection of Christ. We must demand that our politics decree order, justice and freedom for all. We are to expect that our law reflect Biblical and natural law and not be steered by current events and case law but by the law set forth via the Constitution of the United States through the Bill of Rights. Our sociological ideologies must reflect traditional Christian morals and values. Our psychology should be shrouded in the belief of separation of body and spirit with a serious understanding and belief in the supernatural world of things yet unseen for this life is a spiritual journey in which Jesus instructed to "live in the spirit, not in the flesh."

A Christian belief of biology should be one that reflects the creation of man by a Holy God who made each animal on earth to multiply each after its own kind. Our ethics and philosophies must be based on moral absolutes and our theology centered on the theism of one God in three persons reflected by the Father, the Son and the Holy Spirit and the forgiveness of sin for all humans. Finally, our economics, as Christians, must be based on the stewardship of property that we have been entrusted with in which debt is a sin. If you have stuff you can't afford, it is because you may not have been blessed to have it. Living in debt to have things you can't afford is simply wrong and not what God had in mind for us. Getting that idea across to the reader is what this work has tried to accomplish.

It has been my goal to expose the evil that has entrapped each of us into a snare of lies and create a path to truth where your personal financial life is concerned. These are God's principles, and I have been somewhat repetitious and critical for a reason in my attempt to create the foundation needed for a shift in your thinking. Our first step on the journey for truth is to recognize it as absolute. Webster's dictionary defines truth as "conformity to fact or reality; exact accordance with that which is, or has been, or shall be; we rely on the truth of the scriptural prophecies." Yes, this is from Webster's dictionary published in 1828. We certainly wouldn't find that in a modern dictionary, would we? But how much truth do we know in our modern world anyway?

Christ was radical when he walked upon the earth. Your pathway out of debt must be radical. You must get extreme if you are going to succeed in the goal. If not, the world financial beast will reabsorb you into its web of deception and reality of perpetual debt. You will not outsmart this system on your own. It is too powerful, too organized, too cunning and too big.

You must know there is a beast among us spawned from the father of lies. It has no name, no face and no person, but it lives and breathes amongst us. It is anti-Christ and unholy in all its ways, and it deceives, devours our hopes, and creates an atmosphere of fear and dependence upon its philosophies. It is cold and alluring, contemptuous and foreboding. It is careless and uncaring and insidious in its very nature. Conceived in iniquity and born in sin, it is unfeeling and daunting and it lives, devours and enslaves. We must know it, see it, and recognize it by its rotten fruit and its deception. It appears as an angel of light yet the righteous can smell it's stench a mile away. The uninformed will be devoured by it, the unfaithful deceived by it and the foolish will wear its mark all the while believing themselves free men, full of knowledge and enlightenment of this day and age as they prosper from it.

The average American has become faithless, soft, and for the most part, spiritually lazy. Like sheep we follow a ruthless system of materialism designed to make us fat for the slaughter. We want stuff so we purchase, all the while never finding satisfaction in our material world. We have abandoned our hope found in the spirit for the lies of the insatiable flesh. We thirst yet we cannot quench, we hunger yet cannot fill our bellies in this place. There is much more to this life than materialism because this life and this world will pass away, but the word of God will last forever. The world gives us lies, Christ allows us to drink from the well of the everlasting waters of truth.

Christ came as a "testament to the truth." The world we live in is an illusion, a world of vast boundaries and physical laws that have serious consequences when broken. This world is not reality. There is a spiritual realm which our eyes are not designed to see. We live in a sub-set of that reality, and that sub-set will pass away. Therefore, we are to build up our riches in heaven in hope of things yet seen.

Christ tells us that he came that we may not only have life, but have it abundantly. To do so we must live in the spirit through His gospel, not in the flesh of our sinful nature.

A material life leads to emptiness. Each of us will come to an end in this life, as will our parents and our children and their children. Author John Ortberg wrote a book called <u>When the Game is Over, It All Goes Back in the Box</u>. In the book he explains how his grandmother taught him how to play the game Monopoly. She would always win, regardless. She was ruthless in skill at the game as she would quickly gobble up everything on the board and force everyone into bankruptcy. Then, one summer, he played the game every day until he became more ruthless than his grandmother in which he finally defeated her. She then taught him a very valuable lesson. She told him, "Now that you have learned to be successful by obtaining everything possible, it all goes back in the box." The point is, think about what is really important in your life because in the end, all you have managed to obtain in life will mean nothing. It will all go back in the box. All the houses, land, automobiles, titles, recognition, significance, and properties, as well as all the materialistic reflections of success all go back in the box. Game over. You will take none of it with you.

The happiest times of my life were when I was young and poor. Not because I was ignorant or lived in poverty. That was not good. What was good was the fact that everyone in my life was where they were supposed to be. They were alive and we were friends and family, so being poor wasn't much of an issue because we had love. I will always remember the love of my grandparents, the comforts and safe haven of a loving home. I miss them. I miss the relationships, and no monetary object will ever replace those we hold so dear. Perhaps giving up the rat race for the sake of your children wouldn't be a bad thing and could possibly teach them what is really important in life. My brother once told me he wanted his children to have a better life than he did. I reminded him that it was a hard life, and his ability to meet it head-on that made him the remarkable man he was.

Now I will leave you with a stern warning. The world of our fathers is disappearing and a new world order is here, like it or not. Your government through decades of special interest influence of world banking powers will be part of that new world order, as will your education system, your corporations, your media and possibly your church along with everything else you have taken for granted over the course of your life. That new order began by enslaving you with perpetual debt. As a Christian, you may be forced to make serious choices that could land you at odds with this new order. It will be your choice to take a stand or succumb to the beast. Most importantly, remember the words of St. Paul, *"Take up the whole armor of God that you may be able to withstand the evil day, and having done all, to stand."*

I wish you strength, courage and ability. And remember the words of Christ when Peter asked him about death: *"Rejoice Peter, for I have defeated death."* There is nothing to fear as long as you have faith because Christ promised he would be with us always, even unto the end. Godspeed my friend and know, with faith in Christ, you are never alone no matter what happens.

I can only be assured that all the technical information here has been taken from the most respected sources and assembled in the most educational way and that the truth has been delivered to the best of my knowledge. I am a Christian, and the word of God is obviously spelled out in this work. I only want the best for anyone who takes the time to read these ramblings which I have delivered on an 8th grade level as to leave no one confused or misunderstanding of its content. There is knowledge here, and I believe you could really put it to use, but what do I know? I'm just a regular guy, but this is the way I see it!

Resources

Biblical reference taken from The New King James Version; Life Application Bible and The Holy Bible, New Revised Standard:

"The New King James Version", Life Application Bible. Tyndale House Publishers, Inc. Wheaton, Illinois (1993)

"The Holy Bible", The New Revised Standard Version; Thomas Nelson Publishers. Nashville, Tennessee (1989) by the Division of Christian Education by the National Council of the Churches of Christ in the United States of America.

"Rules for Radicals", A Practical Primer for Realistic Radicals; by Saul D. Alinsky [paperback] Publisher, Vintage Books, a Division of Random House, Inc. New York, {1971}

"The Last Chance Millionaire", by Douglas R. Andrew [hardcover] Published by Warner Brothers Books; New York – Boston {2007}

"The Automatic Millionaire" by David Back [paperback] Publisher Broadway Books, New York {2006}

"The Bait of Satan", Living Free from the Deadly Trap of Offense; by John Bevere [paperback] Published by Charioma House, Lake Mary, Florida; {2004} Revised Edition

"The New Jewish Encyclopedia", edited by David Bridger & Samuel Wolk; Forwarded by Abba Eban, [hardcover], updated from the Jewish Encyclopedia 1905

"Big Fat Lies", Advertising Tricks; by John Burstein {March 15, 2008) [paperback]

American Chronicle online Magazine; "Evils of Advertising", by Make Catherall {November 2010}, www.americanchronicle.com

"The Wealthy Barber", Everyone's Common Sense Guide to Becoming Financially Independent; by David Chilton [paperback] 2nd Edition, Prima Publishing {1996}

"Woodrow Wilson: A Biography", by John Milton Cooper, {November 3, 2009} publisher; DeckleHedge; [hardcover]

"The 5 Lessons a Millionaire Taught Me about Life & Wealth", by Richard Paul Evans [hardcover] Published by Simon and Schuster, New York {2006}

"The Creature from Jekyll Island", A Second Look at the Federal Reserve Bank, by G. Edward Griffen; publisher American Media; 13th printing {Jan 2005} [paperback]

"Descent into Slavery", by Des Griffen; a chronicled look into the design of the Federal Reserve Bank. {June 1980}, [paperback]

"The Fourth Reich of the Rich", by Des Griffen {December 1998), Mass Market Paperback, [paperback]

"The Invisible War"; by Chip Ingram [hardcover] Published by Baker Books, Grand Rapids, Michigan {2006}

"The Reason for God", Belief in an Age of Skepticism; by Timothy Keller [hardcover] Published by Penguin Group, New York, New York {2008}

"Un-Christian", What a New Generation Really Thinks about Christianity; by David Kinnaman & Gabe Lyons [hardcover] Published by Baker Books, Grand Rapids, Michigan {2006}

"Rich Dad, Poor Dad", by Robert T. Kiyosaki with Sharon L. Lechter, CPA; Warner Business Books, New York, London; [paperback] {1998}

"Buyology, The Truth & Lies About Why We Buy" by Martin Lindstrom and Paco Underhill {February 2, 2010} Publisher, Broadway Books [paperback]

"Travelling Light", Releasing the Burdens You Were Never Intended to Bear; by Max Lucado [paperback] Published By Thomas Nelson, New York, Boston, Nashville, Dallas, Mexico City Rio and Beijing {2001}

"The Truth War", Fighting for Certainty in an Age of Deception; by John MacAuthur [hardcover] Published by Thomas Nelson, New York, Boston, Nashville, Dallas, Mexico City, Rio and Beijing {2007}

"The Gospel According to Jesus", What is Authentic Faith? By John MacAuthur [hardcover] Publisher Zondervan Books {2008}

"Soul Cravings", by Erwin Raphael McManus [hardcover] Published by Thomas Nelson, New York, Boston, Nashville, Dallas, Mexico City, Rio and Beijing {2006}

"The Rothschild's" Portrait of a Dynasty; by Frederick Morton, Publisher Kadansha-America, Inc. 1961; [paperback] {September 1998}

"The Secrets of the Federal Reserve", by Eustace Clerence Mullins {June 22, 2009} [paperback]

"The 9 Steps to Financial Freedom", Practical and Spiritual Steps So You Can Stop Worrying; by Suze Orman [paperback] Three Rivers Press, New York; 3rd Edition {2006}

"When The Game Is Over, It All Goes Back In The Box", by John Ortberg [hardcover] Publisher, Zondervan, Grand Rapids, Michigan {2007}

"Wide Open Spaces", Beyond Paint by Numbers Christianity; by Jim Palmer [paperback] Publisher Thomas Nelson, New York, Boston, Nashville, Dallas, Mexico City, Rio and Beijing {2007}

"Financial Armageddon" – Protecting Your Future from Four Impending Catastrophies; by Michael J. Panzner [hardcover], Kaplan Publishing; 2007

"The Road Less Travelled", A New Psychology of Love, Traditional Values and Spiritual Growth; by Dr. M. Scott Peck {1985} [paperback] Publisher, Simon & Schuster, New York; a Touchstone book

"What Jesus Demands from the World"; by John Piper [hardcover] Good News Publishers, Wheaton Illinois {2006}

"Financial Peace Revisted" by Dave Ramsey [hardcover] Lambo Press, {1992, 1995 & 2004} Published by Penguin Putnam Inc.

"More Than Enough", The 10 Keys to Changing Your Financial Destiny; by Dave Ramsey [paperback] Publisher, Penguin Books {1999}

"The Total Money Makeover", A Proven Plan for Financial Fitness by Dave Ramsey [hardcover] Thomas Nelson Publishers, Nashville, Tennessee {2003}

"The Richest Man Who Ever Lived", King Solomon's Secrets to Success, Wealth and Happiness; by Steven K. Scott [hardcover] Publisher, Double Day of Random House {2006}

"The 10 Top Distinctions Between Millionaires and the Middle Class" by Keith Cameron Smith; [hardcover] Ballantine books, New York, N.Y., {2007} Random House Inc.

"Truth, Lies & Advertising", The Art of Account Planning; by Jon Steel, {March 13, 1998} [hardcover]

"The Rules of Money", How to Make It and How to Hold Onto It; by Richard Templar [paperback] Pearson Ed, Inc. Published by FT Press, New Jersey {2007}

"All Your Worth", The Ultimate Lifetime Money Plan; [hardcover] Elizabeth Warren and Amelia Warren Tyagi. (March 1, 2005). New York

"The Two Income Trap" Why Middle-Class Parents Are Going Broke [paperback] Elizabeth Warren and Amelia Warren Tyagi.

"The Federal Reserve System" A History by Donald R. Wells {August 2004} [paperback]

News Publications

"Where Did the Bailout Money Go" Dateline NBC Special Report by Chris Hansen; Broadcast in March 2009

"Foreclosures Hit 50 Year High", Bloomberg News; report by Kathleen M. Howley, televised on September 10, 2002

"Some Worry Housing", Foundation for Economic Growth Could Crumble, ABC News commentary by Ramona Schindelheim; Special Report, May 24, 2002

"Where Did the Bailout Money Go" ABC 2020 Special Report by John Stossel, original broadcast December 19, 2008

Wikipedia Information

Wikipedia; Nelson Wilmarth Aldrich, 1841 – 1915, US Senator and Statesman, politician, (en.wikipedia.org/wiki/Nelson_W_Aldrich)

Wikipedia, BANK (en.wikipedia.org/wiki/Banking_Sytem)

"The Rothschild's Family", Visiting the Nation the Rothschild's Built. Wikipedia 2010, The Free Encyclopedia; (enwikipedia.org/wiki/Rothschild_Family)

Wikipedia: Robert Oppenheimer, http://es.wikipedia.org/wiki/Robert_Oppenheimer

Wikipedia: William the 1st, Elector of Hess; Biography, (en.wikipedia.org/wiki/William_1_Elector_of_Hess)

Wikipedia: "The Napoleonic Wars", 1803 to 1815; (en.wikipedia.org/wiki/Napoleonic_War)

Wikipedia: "Woodrow Wilson", 1856 – 1924; (en.wikipedia.org/wiki/Woodrow_Wilson)

Wikipedia; Josiah Stamp, 1st Baron Stamp, Public Servant, England, (en.wikipedia.org/wiki/Josiah_Stamp_1st_Baron_Stamp)

Wikipedia: Derivative (Finance) (en.wikipedia.org/wiki/Derivative_(finance)

Wikipedia; Andrew Mark Cuomo; Governor of New York, 6th State Attorney General, 11th US Secretary of Housing and Urban Development (en.wikipedia.org/wiki/Andrew_M_Cuomo)

Misc Web Sources

Information from Answers; website: informationfromanswers.com; The Rothschild's

"The Rothschild's Bloodline", Visiting the Nation the Rothschild's Built; www.forbiddenknowledge.com/hardtruth/the_rothchilds

"The Judeo-Masonic Conspiracy", The Rothschild's Family (How the Bankers Took Over the World), Website blog; {September 2010}, Author unknown

HubPages, "Mayer Amschel Bauer changed his name from Bauer to Rothschild and became the founding father of International Finance", by thecounterpunch; (hubpages.com/hub/Mayer_Amschel_Bauer)

Texas Historical Site Atlas Page; State Historical Markers, Citizen's National Bank, Weatherford, Texas, 1888; reference to J.R. Couts, (atlas. thc.state.tx.us) Texas Historical Commission"The Modern Banking System" 2010, (www.timeenoughforlove.org/ModernBanking.httm)

Gramm-Leach-Bliley Act of 1999; Disclosure of Non-Public Personal Information; 15 USC, subchapter 1, section 6801 – 6809

HR (House Rule) 5660; Commodity Exchange Act (Commodities Futures Modernization Act) of 2000

INCOME STATISTICS/Business.gov; "The Official Business Link to the US Government, www.business.gov/manage/business-data/income_statistics.html

United States Census Bureau, {January 5, 2011}, "Income Statistics", Guidance about Sources & Historical Income Tables; www.census.gov/hhes/www/income.html

Federal Statistics {March 2007}, www.fedstats.gov